The Power of Divine Eros

Books by A. H. Almaas

Essence with The Elixir of Enlightenment:
The Diamond Approach to Inner Realization
Facets of Unity: *The Enneagram of Holy Ideas*
The Inner Journey Home: *Soul's Realization of the Unity of Reality*
Luminous Night's Journey: *An Autobiographical Fragment*

Diamond Mind Series

Volume 1. The Void: *Inner Spaciousness and Ego Structure*
Volume 2. The Pearl Beyond Price: *Integration of Personality into Being:
An Object Relations Approach*
Volume 3. The Point of Existence: *Transformations of Narcissism
in Self-Realization*

Diamond Heart Series

Book One. Elements of the Real in Man
Book Two. The Freedom to Be
Book Three. Being and the Meaning of Life
Book Four. Indestructible Innocence
Book Five. Inexhaustible Mystery

Diamond Body Series

Spacecruiser Inquiry: *True Guidance for the Inner Journey*
Brilliancy: *The Essence of Intelligence*
The Unfolding Now: *Realizing Your True Nature through
the Practice of Presence*

For more information on A. H. Almaas and all of his publications,
please go to www.ahalmaas.com.

The Power *of* Divine Eros

The Illuminating Force of Love
in Everyday Life

A. H. Almaas *&* Karen Johnson

SHAMBHALA
Boston & London
2013

Shambhala Publications, Inc.
Horticultural Hall
300 Massachusetts Avenue
Boston, Massachusetts 02115
www.shambhala.com

9 8 7 6 5 4 3 2 1

First Edition
Printed in the United States of America

♾ This edition is printed on acid-free paper that meets
the American National Standards Institute z39.48 Standard.
♻ This book is printed on 30% postconsumer recycled paper.
For more information please visit www.shambhala.com.

Distributed in the United States by Random House, Inc.,
and in Canada by Random House of Canada Ltd

Designed by James D. Skatges

Library of Congress Cataloging-in-Publication Data

Almaas, A. H.
The power of divine eros: the illuminating force of love in
everyday life / A. H. Almaas and Karen Johnson.—1st ed.
pages cm
Includes index.
ISBN 978-1-61180-083-8 (pbk.: alk. paper)
1. Love—Religious aspects—Ridhwan Foundation.
2. Spiritual life—Ridhwan Foundation.
3. Ridhwan Foundation—Doctrines. I. Title.
BP605.R53A475 2013
204'.4—dc23
2013004112

Dedicated to my dear husband, Gregory,
whose love of earth and spirit has enriched
the love and life we share.

—KAREN JOHNSON

Dedicated to my wife, Marie, with love and gratitude
for her steady love, love of the truth, delight in life,
and the support and space for me to pursue
both my inner work and the work of birthing the teaching.

—HAMEED ALI

Contents

Music Meditation Selections　ix

Editor's Preface　xi

Acknowledgments　xv

Introduction　1

1. Eros　9
2. Two Loves　31
3. Two Worlds　51
4. One Desire　71
5. Personal Relationships　93
6. The Relational Field　107
7. Sexual Love　135
8. Desire for Union　159
9. Magnetic Love　181
10. Sexy Angel　201

About the Diamond Approach　227

Index　229

Music Meditation Selections

"Adagio molto expressivo" from Beethoven's *Spring* Sonata (Violin Sonata No. 5 in F major, op. 24)   49

"Theme" from the album *Rome: Music from the HBO Series* (soundtrack CD by Jeff Beal)   91

The aria "Ebben? Ne andrò lontana" from act 1 of Alfredo Catalani's opera *La Wally* (sung by Wilhelmenia Wiggins Fernandez on the soundtrack CD of the movie *Diva*)   132

"Niobe's Theme" and "Cleopatra Seduces Caesar," from the album *Rome: Music from the HBO Series* (soundtrack CD by Jeff Beal)   156

"Cleopatra Seduces Caesar," from the album *Rome: Music from the HBO Series* (soundtrack CD by Jeff Beal)   160

"Noche Gaditana" from the album *Suite Andalouse* by Pedro Soler and Renaud Garcia-Fons   199

Editor's Preface

The book you are about to read will usher you into a mystical world hidden in the midst of your everyday life. Led by two intrepid spiritual explorers, this journey embarks from Amsterdam and arrives in the heart of the human soul. The particular quest is to discover the nature of divine eros—the source and the expression of the sublime animal and the sexy angel that lives within each of us. As it uncovers and addresses the age-old misunderstanding that our divine and our erotic natures are incompatible opposites, *The Power of Divine Eros* begins the process of delicious discovery of the reality that unites them.

A. H. Almaas (Hameed) and Karen Johnson have been colleagues and fellow travelers of the inner realms for more than thirty-five years. During this time, Hameed has articulated in more than a dozen books the spiritual path of inner realization called the Diamond Approach. This path has arisen mainly out of their joint exploration and is embodied in the Ridhwan School, a spiritual home for more than four thousand dedicated practitioners worldwide.

Since 2007, Hameed and Karen have taken their teaching on the road in the form of five-day workshops called Quasar Seminars, presenting the Diamond Approach work to new audiences in major cities in Europe and the United States. These public workshops provide the opportunity of direct engagement for seekers who cannot devote the time and energy to a more consistent participation in the Ridhwan School. Each year, Karen and Hameed choose a different city and a different topic that addresses the perennial hunger in the human soul for authentic depth and fundamental realness in personal experience.

The Quasar Seminar from 2008 gave birth to this book as a way to offer you, as a reader, the opportunity to discover some of the preciousness of what is possible for a human being living the experience of divine eros. In the process of reading this volume, you will learn specific practices that support the continuing development of the soul. In addition, those of you who are already following a particular path with its own practices might discover support for these practices through this teaching, specifically through learning how to inquire into your own experience.

Two things set *The Power of Divine Eros* apart from other Diamond Approach books. The first is Hameed's collaboration with Karen Johnson. Karen's passionate and dynamic energy adds a new element to the presentation of this spiritual teaching. She speaks from the same source but with a different taste, a zesty flavor all her own. Their two voices are woven through the book and the teaching, bringing greater illumination and more sparkle to this juicy, evocative material. Hameed and Karen alternated teaching the segments, each of which has become a chapter in the volume, beginning with Hameed presenting the first one. In the session that appears in this book as the final chapter, they both led the discussion that brings the seminar to a close.

The second new element is the fact that *The Power of Divine Eros* presents a more immersive experience of the actual teaching process than any other book by Almaas. Several of his previous books are also based on live teachings, and they include question-and-answer interchanges with participants as well as exploration sessions—exercises modified so that as you read, you can actively engage with the teaching.

In addition, this book includes more of the elements that comprise the full seminar process: The first chapter provides a detailed description of the Kath meditation practice used throughout the seminar. In subsequent chapters, different chant and sound practices are presented. Music meditations were done several times in conjunction with the teaching, and we have specified the musical selections used so that you can listen to these if you like and further enhance your experience. And finally, you will learn a special form of dyadic exploration that you can do if you choose to engage the practices in this book with a friend.

All of these different expressions of the teaching field will enhance the opportunity provided here to experience your own journey of divine eros in a way that is the closest thing—in book form—to being in the seminar room yourself.

Given our desire to pass on as much as possible the living experience of this Diamond Approach teaching, be aware that the resulting book is a hybrid animal: neither a straight transcript nor a book solely devoted to the reader. Because of this, there may be moments when you find yourself drawn into the meeting room in Amsterdam no matter where you are reading the book. The authors trust that you will appreciate being spoken to as the actual participants were in the seminar, while having enough modifications in the material to make it fully relevant for you as a reader.

BYRON BROWN
Editor

Acknowledgments

To all of our Divine Eros seminar participants, who brought such an adventurous spirit to the inquiry so that the seminar took off with great vigor—and only got deeper and more expanded from there—we are grateful. Your heartfelt interest in the truth of your experience opened and developed the field in such a way that we were all transported to new levels of consciousness through its intelligent momentum.

We would also like to acknowledge the skillful work and generous support of our staff, our assistants, and our sound crew, all of whom were instrumental in this event becoming a smooth, unfolding transmission of the teaching. And thank you, Amsterdam, for opening your arms and providing the perfect holding for this event.

The thankfulness we feel in being able to provide this work to the public in book form would not be complete without a deep bow of respect to our editors, Byron Brown and Elianne Obadia. Their patience, clarity, intelligence, and kindness birthed the spoken word into the written and kept the original energy of teaching alive and sparkling. Their work was completed by the care and attention of Liz Shaw at Shambhala in shepherding the book through the publication process.

Last but not least, deep gratitude to the secret essence that bestows upon the world all gifts so effortlessly and generously, through its emissary, the diamond guidance, the particular guidance of this teaching, which enables the beauty, grace, and intelligent unfolding of this teaching so that the soul of humanity might taste its natural freedom.

The Power of Divine Eros

Introduction

IN OUR TIMES, the understanding of spirit and matter is undergoing yet another renaissance, and attempts are being made to bring together many of the variables in human life that keep us separated from ourselves, our nature, and from one another. In this book, we want to share with the reader a way that freedom manifests as a possibility for human beings that is rarely considered or spoken of—the realization that the erotic and the spiritual are not separate at all. That, in fact, they are two sides of the same reality.

The conventional view that the divine and the erotic are separate is necessarily challenged when one opens to the energy, aliveness, spontaneity, and zest of lusty love and finds it inseparable from the realm of the holy and sacred, the pure and innocent. For the ego, bringing these "opposites" together is understood to be disharmonious and paradoxical, at best. However, living a life that separates these fundamental truths of our experience from one another actually perpetuates the suffering that results from the truncated reality of ego existence.

The ideas in this book were originally presented over the course of a five-day seminar that took place in Amsterdam in May 2008, a seminar that we called Divine Eros. We hope that offering this teaching in published form can add to the currents of thought that are carrying us closer to the integration that is possible for every one of us to experience.

A Marriage Made in Heaven

The perspective that the erotic and the spiritual can be wedded in a way that enhances our spiritual journey at the same time as it enriches our personal lives may not be immediately apparent. The erotic and the divine are most often not even seen as complementary in their quality or focus of interest. In fact, the usual human preoccupation with one often cancels the other out, so the possibility of a sacred marriage between the two is rarely contemplated, much less realized. In the course of the seminar, the recognition—and the actual experience—that this cancellation is not necessary was exciting and deeply fulfilling for many of the participants. In fact, the amazing energetic opening and joy during the seminar indicated that the teaching had landed, and inspired us to make it public. Such success showed us the human need for this view and the amazing potential for enhancing our lives when this view is realized.

What emerged for the participants in this seminar—and, we hope, for the readers of this book—is the recognition that the bringing together of our animalistic impulses with the angelic sacredness of our spiritual nature in our human experience can contribute to the journey toward wholeness. We can live fully as physical beings on Earth, inseparable from knowing ourselves as the exalted transcendent truth of spirit. The integration of these levels of existence will allow us to experience the dynamic living presence of our spiritual nature pouring into the world, taking on form and living through that form as who we are in our uniqueness—all the while never stopping being the totality of all.

The Quasar Seminars

In groups and seminars, the work that developed through us and that we have been teaching, known as the Diamond Approach, usually focuses on one specific pure aspect of our spiritual nature as it relates to personal life. We guide the participants toward the realization of that aspect as they work through their ego structures. However, in the Quasar Seminars—this Amsterdam seminar was one of them—which we have taught together in Europe and in the United States for the past several years, we have taken a different approach. Instead of focusing on spiritual aspects or dimensions, we chose themes that enabled us to explore topics of general interest in most people's lives that, at the same time, encompass many aspects and dimensions of our spiritual nature. What we discovered is that this approach spoke to individuals with varying levels of interest and spiritual experience; hence we imagine it will be applicable to a wider reading audience.

While the Quasar Seminars have focused on being relevant to everyday life and its challenges, the various themes that we have chosen also directly relate to the realization of transcendent spiritual dimensions of experience. We see these as two sides of the same coin, separated only by the conventional view of reality that excludes the unknown or invisible world.

As always in our work, we invited the participants to explore their individual experience as a doorway to understanding, making the work a very personal journey that kept each person connected to where he or she was moment to moment in opening to deeper spirit. One reflection of this process is in the question-and-answer periods during which we interact with individual participants; these are included in each of the chapters. And the topics we taught invited exploration of familiar but seldom-discussed areas of personal experience, such as heartfully erotic love toward the inner beloved, how intimate friendship reflects the true beloved, and what it is that underlies real relationships the world over.

While reflecting this universality, the choice of themes for the various Quasar groups has also been related to the location in which the seminar took place; we have found that having discussions with individuals from the country or city where a seminar takes place is useful for pinpointing what is most relevant to a specific time and place. In Amsterdam, the lively interest in the connection between the erotic and the spiritual, the question of sexuality versus religion, led us to the theme of divine eros. We felt that this theme would mesh well with the currents being expressed in the cultural discourse of the time in that city. Many of the people we know and met there are open and full of zesty sparkle, and we realized that their interests could be used to address a hot topic in the community as a means to awakening to reality. So we approached the work of spiritual realization in the group from this perspective. And conditions for our exploration were close to perfect.

Culture and Nature Working Together

The space where the seminar was conducted was called the Rode Hoed—Dutch meaning "red head." At one time, it had been a hidden church, its existence kept secret because it was illegal to practice the Protestant religion. An interesting coincidence, perhaps, that a seminar concerning the hidden secrets of the divine erotic was being held in a place that once held secret meetings of worship. From the outside, the Rode Hoed had the appearance of a lovely historic Amsterdam building. Opening the door, we saw the simple and clean entrance, a greeting room with a small snack bar on the right, ticket counters to the left, and a coatroom farther on.

The double doors at the end of the long entryway beckoned us toward them, and as we walked through these, a whole world seemed to open up. The historical legacy of the old church sanctuary seemed to hang lightly in the air but with no hint of repression. The spacious and elegant feel was, in fact, inviting—containing without any constraint. The dais, a large square area in the middle surrounded by three floors of balconies, felt spacious and welcoming. The old wood, everywhere present, smelled aged and seasoned.

The room was perfect in its dimensionality, supportive and embracing for both the teaching and the energetic field that we created together. The structure of the hall provided a function for us that we had not anticipated: With three levels of balcony seating on three sides, it was like a 3-D teaching space. The most remarkable presence could be felt as soon as the hall started to fill with participants. And the experience of sitting on the dais felt like being surrounded by living angels.

The weather was also of the perfect order. On all five days, it was sunny, bright, and mild. The residents of Amsterdam tend to get even more joyous than usual when the spring weather is that good, so a particularly open and celebrative atmosphere in the city surrounded our meetings. Both local and out-of-town participants enjoyed the whole situation as they delved deeply into the exciting subject matter of the seminar. Culture and nature worked together to support the energy we were activating; the air was effervescent with delight, and nobody could keep a smile from spreading across their face when stepping outside. The overall atmosphere made it easy to stay alert and focused on the journey—an adventure that began to unfold with an understanding that the work of spiritual realization always involves the element of love, a love that does not exclude the erotic.

The Dance of Mind and Heart

As we look into the nature of how love functions on the different paths to realization, we see that in the more devotional types of spiritual practice, at some point the heart explicitly becomes an ecstatic expression of the union with God, or the Beloved. This ecstasy becomes erotic at times, as in the case of some Christian and Hindu mystics. The spiritual paths of mind and knowledge do not tend to bring in this type of erotic and juicy feel; knowledge and its precision open our experience to new realms, but the love is implicit more than explicit. Similarly, when love is present in a devotional and respectful form, it rarely expresses itself as erotic love.

In the way we usually work, we use the mind's discriminating capacity, the heart's loving nature, *and* the body's precious vehicle of life to go beyond all of these without leaving any of them behind. We do not emphasize one over the other, nor does deeper refinement through our work mean that we transcend these centers of our being; we simply see the natural potential hidden within them all. In the course of our spiritual maturation, each becomes more capable and more fully realized, not less.

Thus we use the mind to go beyond the mind's limitations; we use the capacity of discrimination to reveal subtler levels of mind. But here, the heart's innate love for beauty and truth is a guiding principle: The marriage of heart and mind is a must on this spiritual journey, for it is the segmentation of our experience that keeps them limited and restricted to conventional reality. The love of truth allows the mind to open to new possibilities that mental logic alone cannot reveal or consider entering. And the heart can be clarified of its historical and emotional content through the mind's clarity and precision, making available the energy liberated from the trapped structures of our personal history, so it can nurture and enliven our evolving spiritual development. This is the hidden tantra within the work of this path.

The term "tantra" refers to teachings that use energy for the sake of evolving spiritual being. Energy can be erotic, even sexual, but energy can also be emotional, mental, or simply energy itself. In this seminar, we made explicit the ways in which newly unblocked and released energies can liberate the spirit and reveal deeper mysteries of relationship and love—whether with God, true nature, or another human being.

THE SCINTILLATING JOURNEY IN AMSTERDAM

The path of the Diamond Approach—sometimes referred to as Diamond Heart—is a love affair *par excellence*, where the mind and heart are bonded from the start, although this is not so apparent at the beginning of the journey. Both heart and mind are necessary for opening to truth—the deep desire to know the truth for its own sake and the love for the truth beyond all else. And as our practice of inquiry and meditation is refined over time, it becomes more obvious that the interdependence of mind and heart, and their integration through embodied experience, is vital for the revelation of our true being, for the wisdom of knowing and expressing its true nature. And with the wish to know and the desire to become one with that which we discover, the journey—the love affair—gathers momentum. We increasingly feel as though we were being taken over by a great brilliant force of energetic propulsion, with a direction and fortitude that we could not have imagined from our limited point of view at the start.

Our starting point for this seminar was the understanding that any spiritual work involves the element of love, whether explicitly or implicitly. What we wanted to explore during these days was how the energy and quality of love explicitly open the door to reality and to our deeper nature. The process of discovery in the group revealed that the portal is there for every human being to open; each of us can be fully real and alive in all our interactions. And the erotic, as it is felt and experienced in the body, is a part of that openness, whether it becomes sexual or not. For many reasons, eros has become separated from the pure and the holy, and as a result, it is usually relegated to the domain of the gross and unrefined. But eros is the energy of the divine. As such, it is always divine and pure.

One of the main tenets of the tantric approach as it is taught in our work is to feel whatever we are feeling in any given moment. It is not necessary to either act a feeling out or suppress it. We don't try to change either our feelings or ourselves; instead, we let the energy change us. Not acting out an emotion will eventually lead to the pure energy within it. And understanding the charge that we carry about the feeling will allow the energy to be cleansed of the fixed content of the charged emotion from the past, leaving it pure and clean, simply itself. This energy opens us to the realm of Being where we experience the essence of our being as flowing, dynamic, alive, intelligent presence. Frequently, the liberated energy opens up to a dimension of experience where the explosive and dazzling pulsing thrill becomes foreground, manifesting as the fully alive energy of spirit and life. In this process, we see that the spiritual journey need not be a choice between the various parts of ourselves but, rather, through embracing the totality of our experience, the realization of a personal life of nonattachment without renunciation. Nothing has to be excluded. Then we can know ourselves as our unencumbered essence while enjoying a life of fulfillment.

By the end of the seminar, almost everyone was aglow with this recognition expressed in an erotically scintillating aliveness. There had been difficulties and delights, pain, and pleasure, all of which are the natural conditions of a soul's growing into being. But by the end of our time together, almost three hundred people became one delightful undulating ocean of excited clarity and blissfulness. We had grown to become one fluid body with many currents—each one a unique expression of the wonder of reality, simultaneously interconnected with the rest. Each person, with the distinctive unwinding of his or her consciousness, added a particular flavor and spice to the creative dynamic flowering that occurred in those days together.

The inspiration for writing this book has been many-faceted. First and foremost, our interest in offering this teaching emerged from the deep wish to share the fruits of the work that we have done on our own inner journeys. When one has tasted freedom, there is a natural movement to share with others who may benefit from the gifts of what that freedom has revealed. We hope that this book will provide for the reader an opportunity to taste something of what was experienced in Amsterdam. So with deep love and gratitude, we offer this work to all beings for the sake of our evolution, as a species, toward becoming greater conduits for freedom to express itself in all of its astonishing qualities and dimensions.

KAREN JOHNSON
Berkeley, California
July 31, 2012

I
———

Eros

HAMEED

IN OUR WORK in the Diamond Approach, we do many kinds of meditations and spiritual practices. One of the practices we emphasize is being present, because it is important in so many ways. Most people are lost in time—with memories of the past or plans for the future—and are lost in the mind. Being present means being in your experience in a different way than you normally are as you go about your life—that is, in a less distracted condition that enables you to hear better, receive better, feel yourself better, and be more aware of your experience. When we talk about being present, we mean being fully aware of yourself in this moment—you are here in the situation, in the experience, instead of being lost in time and completely taken over by your concerns. You are present in the moment; you are feeling the moment; you are aware of what is happening in the now.

The practice of presence develops over time so that you also become aware of what is present and who is present. Who is the you that is present? What is the essence of your awareness? The practice of presence becomes an important and significant way of knowing our spiritual nature, of knowing and feeling the deeper dimensions of our Being.

One of the specific practices of presence that we recommend is to sense your body. The body has many centers, and the main ones we work with in the Diamond Approach are the belly center, the heart center, and the head center. The core of the primal energies that make up our life force is located in the lower body, and the belly center is the organizing hub for all of these energies. The belly has an energetic center, an energetic spiritual center. It is located in the center of the belly about three fingers below the navel and, depending on the size of your belly, anywhere from two to five fingers inside. The Japanese call it the *hara* center and the Chinese call it *t'an tien*. We call this point the Kath, a term taken from a Central Asian tradition. The belly center is also the grounding center: Your consciousness is like a tree, and the roots of the tree are in the belly. So we will be referring to this center as both the Kath and the belly center.

Because the belly center is related to the energies of the life force, we often have you sense your belly. As you become more aware of that area, and the belly center becomes more developed, more present, you become more in touch with the raw energies of your life force. Then you can better access what we call instinctual energy—the various energies of your survival, sexual, and social instincts.

During this seminar, we begin each of our meetings with the Kath meditation—a specific meditation on the belly center. Some sessions we will add a salutation, chant, or music meditation as a lead-in to the Kath practice. We use the Kath meditation because the belly center is the main one related to divine eros. It will help you connect to divine eros, so that you become both eros and divine. *[Readers are invited to do the Kath meditation (the belly meditation) on their own for twenty minutes daily and in conjunction with reading each chapter of* The Power of Divine Eros. *Exploring this practice as well as other meditations and practices that are described in this book will help to unfold your own experience as you grow in the awareness of divine eros.—Ed.]*

The Kath Meditation

The Kath meditation is usually done in a sitting position. Using a chair is fine, but any other means of keeping your back straight is okay, too. The mudra (Sanskrit for "hand posture") for this meditation looks like the Taoist yin/yang symbol, with the right hand holding the left hand, the fingers of one hand nesting in the other. This is called a mudra of containment, because it helps you contain your energy within so that it concentrates and can develop and strengthen.

For this meditation, it is best to have the eyes closed. Your mouth can be slightly open or closed, and it is good to have your tongue touching the roof of your mouth, the upper palate.

Begin by paying attention to your breathing. Most people breathe in their chest, but in this meditation you will be breathing in the belly. As you breathe, feel your belly, sense it, as though you were touching it from the inside. With each breath, the belly expands, and as you exhale, the belly gets smaller again. You don't have to take big or deep breaths; just be aware that there is breathing in the belly.

As you become aware of breathing in the belly, begin to concentrate your mind—which means concentrate your awareness, concentrate your attention—at the center of the belly. When you concentrate your attention at that center in the belly, you will not find anything in particular. This meditation is simply a concentration of your attention, of your awareness, of your mind, in that region. You might experience sensations of one kind or another; you might sense some localized presence; energy might build up; you might have various other experiences such as pulsation or heat. But the point is to hold a one-pointed focus on that area throughout the meditation without breaking it.

There will ordinarily be other kinds of inner activity and content as well—thoughts and images arising, external or inner sounds, and so on. Do not try to stop or block the content; do not try to do anything to your thoughts, emotions, memories, or sensations. It is fine that these things happen, but the point is to not let them distract you from your focus. The mental or emotional processes can occur without your taking attention away from the breathing in the belly.

If you fail in your initial attempts (as undoubtedly you will), it does not mean that anything is wrong. It is merely a sign that you haven't done this meditation before or that you've been doing it only for a short time. If you get distracted, if you forget, if you become lost in thoughts or memories or planning—just bring your attention back to the center of the belly the moment you become aware that you've lost your focus. You don't punish yourself. It is a practice, a skill you learn, so of course you don't get it the first time. You are not used to focusing your mind in one place without your concentration being broken, so while you are still new at this, it will be broken over and over again.

Keep attempting to stay focused; every time your concentration breaks and you realize it, bring it back to the same place, remaining aware of the breathing in the belly and focusing at the center of the belly. Continue your meditation for twenty minutes, or more if desired.

We want to practice being present all the time as much as we can, not only during meditation periods. We can continue being aware of the center of the belly during normal everyday activities—for example, while riding a bicycle or cooking a meal. Continue feeling your breathing in the belly, though not necessarily the center of your belly. This is a practice of being present, one way of learning to be present in your experience. It can happen in your sleep as well. You might discover that you are dreaming and that you are aware of your belly in the dream.

ILLUMINATING THE DIVINE

In the Diamond Approach, our orientation is not toward having spiritual experiences. In fact, we are not interested in having any particular type of experience at all. We are interested in actualizing our potential. This means realizing who we are, discovering what the essence of our Being is, continuing to recognize this, continuing being what we are—our spiritual presence, our true nature—and learning how to live as that. It is a profound, meaningful way of living.

So it is not a matter of having a succession of experiences while continuing to be the same person, simply adding on more and more interesting spiritual experiences. No: At some point you learn who you are, what you truly are; and the one who lives your life becomes a different person. There could be other possibilities; you might not even feel like a human being at times, but regardless of the particular form that your being might take at one time or another, you want to be *you*, as fully and completely as possible. For a long time, you don't know who that one is. You say, "Me who?"

At a certain point, you realize that what you are is not different from recognizing the nature of your awareness, the nature of your consciousness. It is what you are. It is the essence of your Being. And the essence or nature of what we are can express itself in what we call spiritual qualities, or spiritual forms, or different kinds of subtle energies.

In this seminar, we are going to focus on a particular way that our nature can be experienced—a specific subtle energy that we will call divine eros. Divine eros refers to a particular quality, a particular energy, a particular way of experiencing the nature of our consciousness. At the same time, it is a way of experiencing, feeling, and knowing our consciousness that becomes significant for being open to the depth of our nature.

All of these modalities are useful in the realization of our nature, which means that understanding divine eros is very important for our enlightenment. We chose divine eros as our subject matter because it is a support for enlightenment; but our focus in this seminar, our orientation, is not only directed toward discovering the nature of consciousness and how to be present as that consciousness. More important, what we will learn and experience here is useful for living life—and it is particularly helpful in our relationships with other human beings. In other words, it brings our realization into the situations of our life.

We want to live as fully and as completely as possible. We are living life anyway, and we might as well live it well. To live it well means more than just eating well or exercising well. It means being completely and authentically ourselves, whether we are eating or riding our bicycle or interacting with another human being.

What we are going to be working with is actually a mysterious form of experience, a very subtle quality and also a secret one. It is something that most people do not experience and do not expect to experience. To most people's way of thinking, eros has to do with the animal or physical part of us. And the divine is certainly not seen as being harmonious with the animal part of our nature.

But we want to learn how to experience a particular kind of spiritual condition—the experience of a purely spiritual presence that is, at the same time, the very nature of eros. That presence, that condition, is completely pure, completely spiritual, in the sense that it has no ego, no self-centeredness, no conditioning. This is what we call divine. At the same time, we want to see how it is actually quite erotic.

We are going to be using the word "divine" in a way that may be a little different than some of you are imagining. The word "divine" is usually connected with God. But people use the word "God" to mean other things as well. For some, "God" means simply the purity and the exquisiteness of the spiritual nature. So instead of saying that something is godly, we will say that it is divine, to make a little distinction, a little difference.

When the word "divine" is used in this teaching, we mean pure egolessness. "Divine" is, in a profound sense, beyond this world; it comes from beyond the physical world as we ordinarily know it. It is not physical and it is not emotional. It is not mental. It's spiritual—but not otherworldly. It is spiritual and without ego.

When we use the word "divine," we also mean something that is subtle. It is refined. We say that it is pure, pure in the sense that it doesn't contain other things in it. It doesn't include our past and our beliefs or our ideas about it. It is our nature that is not touched or contaminated by, not mixed with, our history, our associations, our culture, our preferences or ideas. It is completely pure as simply itself.

But whether you relate "divine" to God or simply to the purity of spiritual nature, we want to include in our usage of the word the purity of the spiritual universe, the egolessness, the selflessness, the utmost subtlety, the utmost transcendence, and the complete freedom from all conditioning. There can be a sense of beauty when we use the word "divine," a sense of exquisiteness, a sense of gracefulness, a sense of magnificence, a sense of heartfulness, a sense of abiding in a deep and selfless type of love.

Something happens in the course of doing spiritual work that is very important on any path: The more we are connected with our spirituality, and the more we are aware of and in touch with our spiritual nature and the spiritual nature of reality and existence, the more our heart manifests what it can be in its true nature. Our heart feels the purity of love, a love that is big, unrestricted, and not self-centered. It is a love that is completely generous, totally giving. That is why divine eros brings out a selfless tenderness in us, an egoless sweetness, a generosity and appreciation that is not limited by anything. When I use the word "divine," I am implying all of that.

THE PARADOX OF DIVINE EROS

We all have a way of experiencing love to one degree or another, at one level or another. We all know the experience of the love that is not "I love this so I am attached to it" but rather love in the sense of giving, of appreciating, of truly recognizing what we love, seeing it for what it is, and experiencing a pleasurable appreciation of it. So when you really love somebody, you are happy to see that person not because it gives you something, but because you see who he or she is—and it is wonderful, it is beautiful, it is good. There is a sense of openness and unrestricted generosity—generosity of heart, generosity of spirit.

At the same time, for most people, this love is usually contrasted with—and in their experience, appears to be opposed to—that which we call passion or passionate desire. One of the main polarities that controls or patterns our lives is the polarity between this open-hearted lovingness on the one hand and, on the other, this wanting, this desire and need, to have something, possess something, get something, which makes love more self-oriented and self-centered.

Most spiritual teachings take the position that spirituality is more about pure lovingness and does not have much to do with desire, with wanting, with passion; desire, wanting, and passion are not seen as spiritual. The concern is that engaging in desire, wanting, and passion will take you more into the world, into the mundane, into the physical, and into egoic life. This position is taken because for most people, that is exactly what happens. It is difficult to think of wanting something without wanting it for oneself. We naturally tend to experience wanting—especially strong desire, passionate wanting—in a way that is more focused on the self, that has a self-centeredness to it.

So we end up having two forces, two tendencies, two manifestations, in our consciousness and in our experience: giving, open, generous love on one hand, and wanting, desire, passion on the other. And these frequently appear to be in opposition to one another. In fact, most people experience them as conflicting forces. For many individuals and in many spiritual teachings, spirituality means—and spiritual development requires—letting go of wanting, letting go of desire, letting go of the world and embracing the spiritual. Only this, they think, will make them more loving, more compassionate, selfless, and ultimately free.

But most human beings have difficulty with that view because to them it means that they have to become some kind of saint: "I'm not sure that becoming free that way is for me. Who wants to be a saint? They don't have much of a life. They're always generous, always giving, and do nothing for themselves. Not only don't you have much of a life, there's not even a thought of having an erotic life!"

We will be exploring how to be passionate and to feel a strong wanting *without* that desire being in conflict with the selfless kind of tenderness, with generous sweetness. We will come to see that there is such a thing as divine eros and that we can experience it. And we will discover how to be open to that possibility and access that dimension of reality.

One in Eternity

You might be seeing why, for many of us, it is difficult to know this possibility because in our mind, in our consciousness, in our lives—and in most of history and philosophy—love and passionate desire have been considered two different, opposing tendencies or forces. We experience those two tendencies as being in opposition, in conflict—or, at best, in some kind of harmony or balance—but they are not usually experienced as one. They feel as though they are going in two different directions.

But a long, long time ago, these two forces were not separate. At a time we cannot remember, they were one. And the interesting thing is that they are still one—but they are one in eternity. What does this mean: "one in eternity"? It means that the two are one in the timelessness of our true nature, in the depth of our spiritual nature. The two are inseparable, primordially inseparable.

So we want to explore here what that actually means. We want to understand that not only can these two forces be harmonized so that they are no longer in conflict; they can be the same thing. They *are* the same thing—they are one force. And it is possible to have that kind of experience, that kind of recognition, because it is so: It is—they are—one.

If we look into the nature of that primordial oneness, we will be able to say that this is the case. "Primordial existence" means that something exists beyond our usual condition, beyond our ordinary mental condition of time and space, beyond our conventional categories of experience. "Primordial" means that something is originally so, it is fundamentally the case, but also that it is the case all the time, not only long ago. It is true that a long time ago, the two were one, but that oneness of long ago survives now as well.

But it survives now primordially, meaning that it is in the origin of our experience.

Our experience right now has an origin, has a depth, has a source, but not in terms of time. That is why I use the term "eternally," which is the equivalent of "at this moment." And "this moment" is beyond the time continuum, which means that it is the very now-ness of our experience.

I use words that sometimes are difficult to understand, such as "primordial" or "eternal"; but they have very specific, clear, definite meanings. "Eternally" doesn't mean "a long time in the future." It means "all time," because it is the *now* of all time. It is the source of time, before we think of time; it is what is now. In that primordial place—the fundamental condition of our awareness that is beyond our history, beyond our thinking of time in terms of past and future—when we go to the essence of our consciousness (which we can know only right now, in the very moment of our being), it is possible to see and to experience that passion and selfless love are the same.

But there is a great deal of stuff in the way of knowing this. Many things in our mind, in our experience, stand in the way. One is the belief of many people on the spiritual path, who, as we have seen, take these to be two separate forces, two opposite experiences: "I have a lot of conflict in my life because I want to be realized, I want to be free, and I don't understand how this realm of wanting and desires, needs, passion, and intensity fits with that." The erotic is but one of these manifestations of instinctual energy. "Divine eros" means that there is a pleasurable experience that has desire, wanting, and passion in it and, at the same time, is totally loving—it is completely love, selflessness, and purity.

What we want to do, then, is to unpack all of this and see: How are we going to experience it? How can we see that it is useful for us, not only for our lives, for our relationships—including our love relationships—but also for our spirituality, for our spiritual development? We want to be able to have some access, some openness, to this little-known dimension of our nature, of our spirit, of our true humanness.

The Practice of Inquiry

We are going to do an exercise now to begin to explore these two forces. A meditation is one kind of exercise or practice, but we do other kinds of exercises and practices that have to do with exploring your experience, looking into it, to find out more about it, to understand it. One of the main practices in the Diamond Approach—and one of the main practices that we will work with in this teaching—is what we call inquiry: You look into your experience and you find what your experience is—which means your sensations, your feelings, your thoughts, your emotions, your memories, and so on. To explore your experience, you need to be aware of it, you need to feel it, be in touch with it, experiencing it as immediately as possible.

Inquiry means that we learn to be spiritual not by pushing away our ordinary experience but by embracing and feeling it more completely than we usually do. In fact, being spiritual *includes* experiencing ourselves and being in touch with our experience as completely as possible because, generally speaking, most of us don't experience ourselves completely. There are limitations, restrictions, on how we normally experience things and how we experience ourselves, including our thoughts, emotions, sensations, tendencies, desires. If we experience all of these fully, and if we really understand them, then we will see that they are the manifestations of our spiritual nature. They themselves will take us across the great divide; they themselves will become windows and entryways into the primordial ground, into eternity.

In our orientation here, we do not throw away anything, we do not push away anything, and we do not try to get rid of anything. We always embrace our experience completely, as completely as possible. Inquiry means being aware of our experience, being present in it, feeling it as completely as possible, and at the same time having a curious mind about it. To inquire is to be interested in not only asking "What am I experiencing?" but also wanting to know "What does it mean? What is it about? Why do I feel this way? What makes me experience this feeling or this emotion or this sensation, or these thoughts? Why am I thinking that way?"

By asking ourselves questions, by exploring, by looking at our experience with a curious, questioning mind and an inquiring attitude, it is possible for our experience to begin to open up and show its meaning, to reveal more parts of itself. It becomes possible for us to begin to understand what is happening: "Oh, I see now. It is somewhat difficult for me to be present here, to feel my belly, because I'm still not fully finished with the last conversation with my girlfriend. I didn't tell her everything that I wanted to tell her. And now I realize that is why I am still not settled—I haven't said what I really felt. I didn't tell her that I want to marry her. So of course, it is difficult for me to be present." This is a pleasant example, but there are many other examples, some not so nice.

Sometimes it is difficult for us to be present, or difficult for us to feel what we are feeling, because there might be fear. "I don't want to fully feel my belly because if I feel it, I will see how scared I am . . . and I am scared because it's possible that I might be losing my job." When you recognize that you are a little agitated because you are scared that you might lose your job, we call that understanding. But that understanding is not just thoughts in your mind; it includes the totality of your experience. As you come to understand the fullness of what you are experiencing, you calm down and you feel a different kind of state. The understanding brings more light, more clarity, more illumination to the experience, and that naturally changes it. It is transformed.

So instead of feeling, "I am scared, and it's because I might lose my job," you now start feeling that you are really angry: "Why are they going to fire *me*? I have been doing such a good job!" So things proceed from feeling agitated to feeling afraid to feeling angry. There is nothing unusual about this progression, but if we are not aware of it, if we don't understand the relationship between all of these feelings, we tend to be unsettled inside. That is because we are not fully in touch with our experience.

In this example, our understanding can go further. "Why am I angry? Yes, I've been doing a good job, but I'm angry that they are going to fire some people and I am going to be one of them." You might start remembering that your father was never happy with your grades in school. When you brought your report card home, maybe there was one B+ on it, and he would always say, "You can do better than that. Next time, bring home all As." And you realize that you are carrying a deep disappointment inside that has a personal history. Because your father didn't recognize that you were doing a good job, and because whatever you did was never enough for him, then whenever there is the slightest indication—even decades later—that somebody is not recognizing your good work, you believe that they are going to be disappointed in you, or even that they are not going to like you.

If you go further and explore the question "Why do I care whether or not my father sees what I'm doing?" you could begin to feel after a while, "Because he is my father. I love him and it was important that he love me." And if you allow that recognition, you might start feeling love—and before you know it you turn into a pink rose. "That's interesting—I'm a pink rose . . . smells very nice." And all these petals are opening and unfolding.

So what started out as an irritation ended in a spiritual experience. That is actually how our consciousness works. If you understand it, it opens up. If you don't understand it, it stays the same.

We want to do an exercise now, an inquiry that is based on this principle of open and curious exploration. When you are doing an inquiry on any topic, alone or with others, you might find certain tendencies within yourself—for example, you could think that there is something wrong with you, or you may want to find fault with yourself or feel bad about yourself. It is important that you look into your experience not from the perspective of thinking that it is good or bad, nor from the perspective of judging it or criticizing yourself, nor from the perspective of finding fault with your experience. You simply want to understand it. You want to discover the truth that is in it. If you find yourself with these tendencies, just become aware of them and include them in the inquiry, without getting identified with them. Be more of an explorer. You are not to be a judge. You really just want to find out.

When you do a practice with others and a discussion at the end is suggested, as much as possible you want to have that same attitude of being open and exploring together. You want to be as mature and open as you can, both with yourself and with others. If everyone takes the attitude of genuinely wanting to explore, of really loving discovering what the truth is and wanting understanding, it is easier to deal with those tendencies.

EXPLORATION SESSION

This exploration will help reveal how you experience the opposition or conflict between the selfless giving of love and the passionate wanting, the two forces discussed earlier. Spend fifteen to twenty minutes considering these questions. If you are doing this exercise alone, you may want to write them down in a journal and respond in writing.

1. How do you experience the selfless giving of love?
2. How do you experience passionate wanting?
3. How do you experience the relationship of the two in your life, in your experience?
4. How do you experience the opposition, the conflict, or the disharmony between the sweet, giving, "spiritual" love on the one hand, and the wanting, the desire, the passion and intensity on the other?

If you are doing the practice with others, you can take turns asking one another these questions and being present for each other as the responses arise. After everyone has finished responding, have a discussion to see what you have discovered. What were the commonalities and differences? Exploring what came up for each person and what the common threads were can give you a deeper perception about this issue, adding more insight, more illumination, to your experience.

This is an emotional exploration, a felt exploration, not an intellectual one. You are not offering theories about the opposition of these forces. You are remembering and describing your actual feelings: "I feel this way . . . I feel that way . . ." You can look into any part of your life, but as you explore those feelings, you might move from incidents or feelings from the past into more of how it is in the present moment. As you see the patterns in your life that relate to conflict or opposition between these two forces, you will begin to be aware of things in the moment that you can include in your inquiry.

QUESTIONS AND COMMENTS

Student: In the inquiry, I had three things that I wanted to talk about: my desire, love, and passion. I am quite puzzled about how I can integrate them.

Hameed: You had three, so it is more complicated. I guess some people had more than two. I was trying to make it simple, but I guess life is complicated like that; we do find such complexity in our experience. Usually in spiritual teachings, passion is put together with desire, in the sense that it is a passionate desire rather than only passion by itself. However, in reality, passion can be with desire or with love. Passion is a quality on its own. It is good that you saw that. The polarity that we are trying to work with is the selfless, giving kind of love—which most people think is not passionate—and desire and wanting, which can become passionate. You might find that the passion becomes fuller at either end. That is a good insight.

———————

Student: You were elaborating about the meaning of the word "divine," and I found that very interesting. I also have a lot of associations with the word "eros." I get that it's "eros" as in "erotic," and

I was wondering where the word "erotic" came from, because that has many associations, too.

Hameed: I haven't discussed that yet, but we will. We definitely will explore the various associations and the meaning of "eros." That is what I was saying: We are putting "divine" and "eros" together, and usually people don't do that. So we want to see *how* can we put these two together. I discussed in some sense the wanting, the desire, and the pleasure that goes with desire, and the activity of desire and wanting. But "eros," as we will see, means much more than that.

Student: I discovered certain contradictions within giving, within passion, and within desire. When I explored the question of giving, I found contradiction because there is, on the one hand, the quality of giving generously and openly, and on the other hand, giving with a strategy, which often is unconscious: I give something while actually wanting to receive something. This polarity is one thing I discovered. Within passion, I saw that when I really become passionate, I become afraid of losing ground and connection, and of becoming kind of like a maniac, maybe. And with the desire, I found out that actually there is fear of showing my desire, fear of being rejected. So, yeah, I saw that these are not really contradictions but different places within myself where these impulses are coming from.

Hameed: You discovered many things that are useful, so that is very good. That is what we want to do. We want to explore our experience and discover all these things, because many of us have difficulties with desire, passion, or love. Usually people think that love is a difficult thing, but sometimes desire is actually more difficult for some people.

Student: Yeah, and I was surprised at how many different subtle levels are in these main contradictions that you spoke about.

Hameed: Yes, there are many levels and degrees, and hopefully we will explore more of that in detail. In most spiritual teachings, the position is that true love is difficult, and there is the assumption that everybody experiences desire and that it is a problem. But if we look into our experience, we see that sometimes desire itself is not easy. And when desire is not easy, eros is limited because eros goes with desire. If there is no desire, Cupid has no arrows.

Student: In our group inquiry, one of the things that we found in common was that there is a constriction in each of us. I found that I was comfortable with desire and selflessness, but when I get in contact with other people it gets confusing; there is almost a boundary that comes up, almost an autistic shell. I can have that selflessness by myself or without a real awareness of being present or in contact with others. So there is a barrier between me and other people. The two other people I worked with—their barrier was with their desire.

Hameed: That is a good and very interesting insight about the question of desire. We are finding out that desire has many conflicts and issues around it. It is not as simple as we might have thought. Before we can be free from our desires, we first need to experience desire, to embrace our desire, which we may find is not easy. But hopefully, Cupid will have enough arrows for all of us. It usually looks as though he only has a few on his back, but I think there is no limit to their number. We will see that there are difficulties in love being true love and in desire being complete desire—and then there is what happens between them!

Part of the conflict between the two is something that makes it difficult to experience desire. Many of us are afraid of our desire because it might affect our love, positively or negatively, and we are afraid of both possibilities—desire can make us love more or it can make us less loving.

Student: Just sitting here, this thought has come up. It touches on your saying that if our desire is limited, perhaps that is affecting us more strongly than if love is limited. Your examples are of quite wholesome desires, but I'm thinking of my desires to be shut off, to not feel. In that case, would I be wanting those desires to have more space? Because actually it is really a desire to cut myself off. I have a strong desire to sort of stay under the radar.

Hameed: So there is a desire for staying under the radar?

Student: Yes.

Hameed: For what purpose? Out of fear, out of wanting privacy, or because you don't want to be noticed?

Student: For mixed motives; sometimes it is for privacy, for calm, for having a clear pool rather than the muddy water of lots of other people's psyches, but at other times out of fear or habit. My question is: Are you including those desires when you talk about desire?

Hameed: We include all desires, but we want to focus at some point on desire in relation to other people. But it is true that desire can happen independent of other people. So desire itself is a whole topic of its own, and we are including in it desire, wanting, wishing—all the dynamic force to go toward something or to bring something toward you. We are all of that. Maybe you have a desire for privacy, you want privacy. Like it is not there and you want it.

How about love? Is the pure divine love easy for everybody here? We've been talking about the difficulty in desire, and it makes me wonder whether perhaps people here don't have a problem with generous, giving, sweet, selfless love. Maybe Amsterdam affects people that way, like the sunlight today.

———————

Student: I just think that we all know this conflict, that in a long life we sometimes have this meeting between desire and what you call generosity of love. But before we get to be disillusioned or pessimistic about it, I think that sometimes we know that these things combine. Very recently, I had the good fortune to fall in love, and here is this Romeo and Juliet situation where the problem actually evaporates, disappears, where you find there is a strong combination between the generosity, the affluence of your mind and your passion. Though there is a conflict, it sometimes disappears, doesn't it?

Hameed: That is what Cupid's arrow does. That is exactly right. It is possible to experience that there is no conflict between the two and that they go together quite well. That is what we want to explore. What is it exactly, that *something* you taste when you are in love, that is so wonderful? That is one reason why people love to be in love. People always want to be in love. Most of the stories that are written are about falling in love.

Student: I was sharing this experience with the group: I recently had an experience where everything stopped and there was something that came up like a fountain.

Hameed: Something came up like a fountain?

Student: Yes, at that moment the only thing I could think of was to go around and kiss everybody.

Hameed: That sounds nice. It must have felt good.

Student: For a minute.

Hameed: You wanted to kiss everybody—why? Did everybody look wonderful? And you felt wonderful too, yeah?

Student: Yes, but I found myself stopping it.

Hameed: Why? Was it too good, or too pleasurable, or did it bring up some fears?

Student: I thought I was going to lose my head, meaning I would get sucked in and I wouldn't be able to get myself out to live a normal everyday life. I would be a crazy person. All I could think of was my husband—if he ever finds out that I felt like kissing another man so passionately, more than him . . .

Hameed: I see; that is the concern. And who knows, if you feel it in yourself, it might be more contagious than you think.

Student: I did notice that.

Hameed: It is very scary; you are right. Many of us are very scared about that. We don't know how to be that way. It is too powerful or strong for us, or we feel it could be overwhelming. How is our mind going to function? How are we going to live our life? What is going to happen to our primary relationship? And all of that.

Everything will be up for question—which is, to me, very good. I think it is good to question everything, don't you think so?

Student: At that moment, it is like this is the force of life, this is it.

Hameed: Is that how the fountain felt?

Student: All the way from my belly . . . it was just gushing up.

Hameed: That is a good thing about the belly meditation, about staying in the belly. That can open up the energy, and then the energy sometimes moves up like that. When you felt it moving up, what did you feel was moving up?

Student: It was a tunnel. It was an empty tunnel.

Hameed: What was moving in the tunnel?

Student: It was erotic, something that makes the whole body tremble, and it feels like a flow. It is just energy. That is the only thing that was dynamic, that was the only thing that was moving.

Hameed: So it is dynamic, a dynamic flow.

Student: Very dynamic.

Hameed: But it made you feel like you wanted to kiss people, which means that it had a feeling to it. It affected your heart in a certain way.

Student: Yes.

Hameed: In what way did it affect your heart?

Student: Everybody looked beautiful.

Hameed: Which made you feel what toward them?

Student: Grateful.

Hameed: Interesting.

Student: Very grateful—grateful for giving me the love. Grateful for loving me the way I am, I think.

Hameed: That is beautiful. There is love and gratitude, seeing the beauty of people. When you see the beauty that is here in people, you can't help but love them; and when you love people, you can't help but see the beauty. That can allow your heart to ripen, become full, and one of the things that arises out of that fullness is gratitude. That is a good opening. You are learning something about yourself.

Student: Thinking back now, every time that memory comes back, my hands get icy, like a block of ice.

Hameed: Just the memory of it?

Student: In the head.

Hameed: Obviously it was challenging for you, and some part of you is reacting to it, getting tense about it. As you said, you get scared. So now you explore that: What is scary about it? What is the fear? What is the reaction? How come I am reacting this way about this thing that felt so beautiful? The inquiry continues.

The inquiry into our ordinary experience can bring up other things, some deeper parts of ourselves. So we continue inquiring, and we will most likely have responses to what we find; then we continue by being interested in those responses and exploring them, too. That is a good example of what inquiry can do.

We see, then, that people are having various kinds of insights and experiences, and all that we have done is to explore something that we normally experience in our lives—two qualities of the heart— love and desire—that we generally consider to be incompatible.

2

Two Loves

KAREN

Before we begin the Kath meditation, we will do an om salutation. Om is considered to be the original vibration, the first sacred mystical sound representing creation and oneness. It originates from the Hindu/Sanskrit tradition, but it is considered sacred by other religions such as Buddhism and Jainism. We do the salutation as a simple bow in which we remember our depth, our source, our true nature, and we dedicate the fruit of our work today to the truth in whatever way Being manifests through us.

To do the salutation, we place our palms together with the fingers up in the prayer position, and then bring our hands up so that they are lightly touching the forehead. Now, all together, we say an om on a long, slow exhale as we bow forward from the waist or the pelvis, whichever is comfortable. When we finish the breath and the bow, we sit back up, release the hands, and assume our position to begin the Kath meditation.

We will continue now with our exploration of this broad topic of divine eros, slowly building on this basic theme to give ourselves the opportunity to immerse ourselves in the subject. As you will see, the division between spirit and eros, or the divine and eros, brings up myriad conflicts within ourselves.

So we invite you to just be with your experience, whatever it might be throughout the process. See what arises as you take in what is being said here. Various thoughts, feelings, responses, reactions, and insights will come up—all of which are part of opening up to new dimensions of experience. And if you are doing the practice exercises with others, be aware of what your responses are to them as they share. Allow all these elements of your experience—embrace them, invite them—and welcome yourself to be wherever you are. On our journey, the crucial element is the way in which we approach our experience. Just be open to yourself, to what you are in touch with, without manipulating yourself internally to try to get to where you think we might be headed.

Our Two Loves

The human heart has two loves. First of all, the heart has a deep love for life. Generally people love life—the fact of being alive. You may not like everything about it; you might like to change some—or even a lot of—the content. You might like to change a few people in it. Nevertheless, as a race, we seem to cherish life; we are interested in life, we want to live a full and fulfilling life and enjoy it.

In addition to all the other kinds of activities and delights that we have, we find our personal relationships very important, near and dear, to us. People differ in the value and emphasis they place on personal relationships, but we can guess that the majority of people do value them. Our children, our spouses and significant others, our friends as well as our families—these are the people we enjoy life with. So there is not only enjoyment of life, but also enjoyment of the people in our lives. As human beings and social creatures, we enjoy loving, we enjoy being loved, we enjoy sharing.

Human beings have these precious experiences with more varied colors and richness than any other species, as far as we know. We are consciously able to develop relationships that continue to open and show great treasures beyond this physical existence. We go through various stages of life, sharing with our friends, acquaintances, and loved ones the things that we are learning, that we are excited about, that we are struggling with. We enjoy sharing whatever we love.

There is another side to us as well. In addition to our relationships, another realm draws the attention of the heart: the love of mystery, the fascination with what might lie beyond our normal view. Since ancient times, human beings have been seeking to know and understand whatever is there. This has expressed itself in many ways—through the adventure and exploration of the external world and how it works, and also through our inner exploration, the quest for meaning and the desire to understand our place in the universe. The question "Who am I?" has been a significant part of our evolutionary story.

All the questions that arise at the beginning of the spiritual journey become more scintillating as we get a taste of what lies beyond and a taste of our spiritual being and its vastness, its magnificence, its beauty, its lightness, its unfettered nature. Each taste tends to inspire love and appreciation, to make more love available in every way; and the love grows and expands both inwardly and outwardly. The more we know about our nature, our spiritual nature, the more we love it, the more it draws us, pulls us. The more we feel the expansion of how we view our life, the more we feel, know, and are drawn by and to a more fundamental sense of reality. As our questions are answered, more questions come to replace them. The unknown grows as we come to know it.

We love the known in our life—this world with all of its limitations and difficulties—but we also love this fascinating mystery that lies beyond our physical, earthly existence, that which is unlimited and completely outside of time and space. "Outside of time and space" doesn't mean that time and space is a bubble that our nature somehow lies beyond and outside of, and this bubble somehow erupts into what lies beyond. What it means is that time and space is a bubble, and our nature pervades it. Time and space is the context in which our lives happen; it is where our relationships occur, where the many and varied individuals that we come in contact with and share life with are born. Our bodies appear within this context, emerge out of what seems to be a very mysterious process of growing and exploding into life within somebody's belly. What a miraculous thing that is.

But where do we come from before this time-space bubble becomes the home for our bodies? What happens before that, or after that, or even throughout it? We usually consider our lives to be precious and beautiful, but that beauty and preciousness are an expression of something more fundamental than this world. The allure of the unknown, which for some of us becomes the spiritual dimension of life, somehow feels outside and far away at first. The heart is pulled toward the enticing realms of its original dwelling place. The more we know and experience what is beyond our conventional emotional level of experience, individual mind, and the physical dimension, the more we begin to encounter a deeper reality and the freedom of Being. We feel how light and unencumbered is its nature, how limpid and lovely it is.

Humans love life. And humans love inner freedom. But we feel these as two loves. We may not conceptualize it that way—we may intellectually hold it that the spiritual world and the physical world are one—but emotionally they are often held as two separate realities. Hence they become conflictual for us in many respects. On the one hand, the experience of spiritual freedom renders us free of limitations that we might have thought were simply part of existence. Yet, even though over a period of time, we begin to feel an inner freedom, we may also feel that something is missing when the other, more "earthly" love is not fulfilled.

Our nature, in its purity, is complete. You can't say that something is missing from it. It encompasses everything because our nature *is* the nature of everything; our experience of fundamental reality does not exclude anything. So when we are in the vastness of the ocean of consciousness, the experience of reality feels transcendent. But we might feel that we are missing something if we don't have relationships. If we're not sharing with another person, we start missing that. How often have you gone on a spiritual retreat and sat for a week, or have gone walking in nature and had an epiphany, and find that you can't wait to go tell your friend what happened? There is something about sharing it, about saying it, about expressing it. There is something about letting other people know that a wonderful thing happened. This thing that happened to you, you want them to know it, too.

So we all want to share what we love. In doing this, we are sharing the very nature of what we are, the very beingness of what is all. We share with others our love for them, but we also want to share this freedom we have that is beyond anything in the world. The question of how to live from this freedom usually presents us with a disparity, puts us in a bind. How do we remain in our experience, unencumbered by worldly concerns—outside the world and its limitations, feeling complete freedom, freedom from all the sorrow and the suffering—and still participate in the world we live in? How can we be free and completely separate from all the limitations that we thought we had and yet be in the world with all of its limits? How to reconcile these two realms, these two loves?

We love our relationships, we love life, we love being in the world. We might not feel it on some days, because living is very frustrating at times, but when push comes to shove, we want to protect our lives, we want to enhance them. We do things to try to nourish ourselves, make ourselves healthy, bring ourselves into greater wellbeing physically, emotionally, and mentally. And we also want our freedom, our delight, our expansiveness; we want to feel our fullness. We want to be authentic, to live in a way that is real and true, but we often feel that we have to get away from the world in order to do that.

We want to be away somewhere on our own, because when we are with people, we feel that we are putting on airs, or that we have to change ourselves inside to be able to relate to them. Even though we love them, even though we want to share with them, we might still feel limited in our expression. We feel that we can't have total freedom and still relate authentically to them. We start to feel restricted and constrained.

So maybe we go on a walk in nature and then we feel free. We don't have to talk to anybody; we can sit and meditate, get in touch with ourselves, feel our expansiveness, feel open and spacious. But after a week of that, the thought arises, "Wouldn't it be nice to go have a glass of wine with my friend?"

We start to miss that other side.

We start to feel that we want to be back in the world again: "I love the world . . . I want to see my kids . . . I want to be with my husband . . ." So we spend time with friends, family, partners, and we feel happy for a while; we have meaningful contact and life seems good. But at some point, we start to feel restricted by that again: "Something is not quite right or complete; I'm missing something. What happened to that freedom? Yeah, it's nice; we are communicating well and things are okay, but what happened to that expansiveness, that vastness, that feeling of freedom and openness I had when I was by myself? I feel limited again." So we have to follow that love back to its origin and enjoy ourselves in a way that gives us that time of inner aloneness when we can be completely expansive.

That's how our heart is. It goes one way, and eventually starts to feel that it is missing something. So it goes the other way and, after a while, it feels that something is missing there, too. It is a constant back and forth.

It might be useful to understand what it is about love that makes our heart respond to these two sides of our nature by making us feel pulled in two seemingly opposite directions. You may recognize yourself in this description because you, too, feel pulled in both directions. You want to feel the ability to have your enjoyment, your delight and zest and love for life, and enjoy that part of yourself—and at the same time, you want to feel your spiritual freedom. How to reconcile these?

Through love.

Love creates a bridge because it is something that we feel toward both of these potentials. If we understand more about what love is, we might see how it provides a connecting link to both these sides of our consciousness. The average human being has all kinds of assumptions and ideas about love. Based on our prior experience, we assume that we know what love is and what it means. We assume that our ideas about love and our feelings of being in love or being loving reflect what there is to know about love. But we might not have the last word on it. We all tend to get trapped in the known and are not open to the unknowns of love anymore.

Love is a very human quality. It is one of the traits that humans share. Most humans experience love of some kind. It is one of the things that humans are sensitive to and need from the beginning of life. In fact, we need it to survive. Without love, we fail to thrive. For babies, without love there is no health, there is no well-being, and little chance for life as we know it.

Even if our understanding of love is limited, we all have a notion of what it is. We all have experienced it and can say how it makes us feel. There are certain things that many might agree about—for instance, that love is sweet. Does anybody think that love is not sweet? Okay, let's say that 99 percent of people think love is sweet. Also, when we think of love, we think of softness. Or we think, "My love can be strong, too." And we always think of love as a kind of goodness as well. So when we think of strong love, it is always good, and it is always sweet, too. So we know love as sweet and soft and strong and good.

Where did everybody get the idea that love is sweet and soft? Where did that come from? The idea is derived from somewhere. Some universal truth—a fundamental reality that underlies everyone's experience—is influencing our ideas of love. We have felt it, we have experienced love in a way that actually felt soft and sweet. And at some point in our life, when the veils are rent and we feel naked to love, when we fall in love, humans get a taste of love beyond the word itself and the nice feeling, or the friendly gesture that comes with it, or the hug that conveys "I love you." We actually taste the sweetness. We feel ourselves melting. We feel the softness. Our bodies actually become a feeling of softness, as if something were welling up from inside and giving us a feeling that love is there.

You know when you are feeling loving and you know when you are not, and you know the difference because you feel it. Love is a state. It is an experience that arises within your consciousness, and it has the feeling of softness. It can be like liquid sweetness flowing through your veins, infusing every cell, and pumping you with a liquid that feels nourishing and sweet. Babies feel the sweetness and softness of love before they ever have the idea of love. They *are* the love.

That is how you originally knew it, and deep inside, you never forget it. It is in your flesh and bones.

Love is the most real thing that many people ever experience. It is usually called to mind as a distant memory, and then it becomes what we call emotional love. But even in the experience of emotional love, we can tell when we like somebody or we don't like somebody. There remains a knowing of some kind. Something happens in the heart. And our body language shows it. One can become more held in and held back when the energetic contraction of dislike exhibits itself. You can notice that the chest is more caved in or protected. In contrast, liking and loving offer up more and more generous movement and openness. As you lean slightly toward another, perhaps the chest softens and the arms release their protective armor. A softer heart and a less defended posture are attributes of love coming through our physical expression. There is a natural moving *toward*, in every way. And almost a glowing.

What is this glow? From where does it arise?

THE PRESENCE OF LOVE

Real love expresses itself in these ways, although we might not actually be aware of its presence in the way that we could. The more we feel love, the more we actually glow with it. When we follow love to its source, we may feel the actual presence of love itself. Then love is no longer just an idea, a thought, or even an emotional affect. We are in touch with the underlying presence of love, which has the feeling of an actual presence of light and fullness. It's almost physical, like a pooling or a liquid, soft presence.

And this is why we do the practice of sensing our belly and breathing into it—because whenever we practice, we can become more present. And we can do that practice in any situation or circumstance; we don't have to set aside a special time.

To become more present means that we're in the now. But being in the now doesn't mean only that we are not distracted, or that our minds are listening, paying attention and focused. Yes, it's helpful when the mind is not lost in all kinds of historical events or future projections, and that provides a good entryway. But when we actually find ourselves present, we are not only in the now in our mind and body, we are also in the now in the sense that we are actually *feeling the presence of now.*

Presence is our spiritual freedom liquefied, condensed. Presence is an actual sense of here-ness—beyond our emotions, beyond the mind, beyond our ideas. In presence, we can know ourselves in a way that is authentic, which means that we are knowing what is real in us. When we feel presence, we are experiencing our underlying reality. It feels more real than the physical, the emotional, or the mental realms of experience. And it can't be defined in any of those terms. So when we feel the presence of love—the actual liquid sweetness and its melting nature, or its fullness and richness and softness—we begin to see that the ways we have known love have been limited.

Some of you may know this feeling yet never conceptualized it as such. You might be saying inside, "Oh my God, yeah, I have felt that; I know that." Sometimes another person needs to point to it and say to you, "Yes, that is real, that is true . . . that is *you.*"

The sweetness, the softness, the pooling, the good feeling, the pleasure and enjoyment, are so rich, and feel so real—undeniably real. And the realness is true for presence of all kinds. We can feel presence in many qualities, but love is one that we have access to emotionally—it has a distinct emotional affect, which many essential qualities don't have (such as clarity and will and strength). And if we find ourselves dipping into the experience of that emotion and feel ourselves, sense ourselves, and let that open up, it will naturally open into that feeling of sweetness, softness, fullness, and richness.

In this place, the heart is not divided. When we know the presence of love, we can actually feel that fullness as an expression of freedom in our personal relationships, *because presence cannot be contained*. In fact, the presence of our nature uses our heart as a way to show itself on a personal level in relating to other people. Our love is not limited, it is not finite, because our heart is not finite. Our heart is hooked up to a very big valve, and that valve can't be turned off. The turnoff is in our own heart. Because we have notions and associations about love, we keep our heart valve mostly turned off and only let our love occasionally trickle through. But if we follow those dribbles back to that big vein, that mother lode, it is natural for our heart to open and flow.

The heart is naturally generous, naturally open. In our natural condition, and when all is working well, love expresses itself in many ways. When the heart is open, it is a sensitive organ that loves because that is what it is here for. Just like the physical heart that keeps sending life into the cells as it pumps blood, our essential heart allows the nectars of our spirit to continuously flow. And we don't have to run around physically hugging people; the heart is capable of hugging someone without their even knowing it.

When we know the nature of love, we can begin to see that, in fact, our spiritual nature is what can embrace our personal relationships. And the richness that happens within a personal relationship, between two people, has a preciousness that helps us to become more and more able to love. Our personal relationships can open us up more, develop us more, and give us the opportunity to be more in touch with the freedom we cherish. But if we don't know what real love is, those things do not happen easily.

The presence of love is the lifeblood of our relational heart. Yet, as we have seen, the heart tends to remain divided—on the one hand, we love our spiritual nature, the freedom, the vastness, the beauty, and the mystery, and on the other hand, we love our worldly activities, enjoyments, and personal relationships. It feels as though the two sides of our precious human being–ness were disparate, separated, and unrelated—the sense that we must choose one over the other. Organized religion, historically, has been one way to attempt to blend daily life with spiritual life: "Okay, I'll take the family to church on Sundays . . ." But all too often, this doesn't really work; the division in the heart between the spiritual and secular is not bridged in actual experience. The result is that the spiritual life is compartmentalized instead of infusing the totality of life.

People whose family life and daily activities were split off from their spirituality during childhood may tend to seek out settings apart from ordinary life in order to experience their spiritual side, as this seems to be the only option. Even if one has not experienced a serious split, it is often difficult for a dedicated practitioner to find a context for serious spiritual study and practice that remains embedded in day-to-day life. This challenge is particularly true in the West, where there is such an emphasis on developing a personal life of relationship and accomplishment that those pursuits seem to be at odds with a compelling interest in spiritual disciplines.

For some people, bridging the split between the religious and the secular manifests as following the dictates of God as interpreted by religious authorities in relation to behavior and lifestyle choices. This can be compelling because it only requires following the rules, but these can easily become confused with parental dictates. When following rules does not emerge from an inner alignment with truth, the will of the superego gets confused with the will of God.

Religions can be of great benefit in this area because they often function through spiritual formulations that are simple and understandable and thereby accessible to many people, but they can be quite limited in other ways. While offering beliefs and guidance for

living, they don't generally provide teachings of the total view of
reality from which the guidance springs, so the experience of the
underlying richness is limited at best.

On the other hand, some spiritual teachings specifically encourage engagement with practice rather than adherence to belief.
When these practices are engaged separately from the demands of
daily life, they enable one to get in touch with the presence of freedom to one degree or another, and to experience and feel in a fundamental way the spaciousness and presence of one's nature. But to
authentically become who and what we are, to know the presence of
that spiritual nature, *and* at the same time to walk in the world, have
our relationships, and enjoy our lives—all as one unified experience—is rare. Still, it is possible.

Throughout our work together, we will be investigating and
understanding for ourselves these areas of our experience—our
spiritual and secular sides—which appear as polarities upon first reflection, to help us identify the common elements in them. To aid in
our exploration of the nature of divine eros, it will be useful to understand the interrelationship of these elements. And ultimately to
recognize that love is both the bridge and the entryway into the center point where these polarities meet.

EXPLORATION SESSION

Let's contemplate a few questions related to this particular subject
matter. In the following exercise, you will explore the specific ways
that you experience your love for the world and your love for spirit,
by inquiring into the situations where those loves come up that you
encounter or are aware of in the world and your ideas and feelings
about them.

Spend fifteen to twenty minutes on this exercise, which can be
done alone in writing or with other people. Sense into your body
and see what sensations arise as you engage this inquiry. See what is
there that you might not have noticed before. Be as spontaneous in

your contemplative questioning as possible to allow things to surface that you might not know or be aware of. Let yourself go beyond what you have known about yourself. Don't try to control anything, manage anything, or manipulate the answers. This is an investigation into your own consciousness to learn more about it and open it up, and that means allowing new content to arise that can lead to new openings and knowing.

Contemplate the following three questions:

1. What are the ways in which you experience your love for the world?
2. How do you experience your love for spiritual freedom?
3. How do you experience the relationship between these two loves?

In contemplating the third question, if you don't experience a relationship between the two loves, that is all you have to recognize. Just keep seeing what else is there about that; let whatever it is come up. If you do experience a relationship, notice the way or ways you feel the two loves as similar. What is it that connects them?

QUESTIONS AND COMMENTS

Student: My mind has this pitted so strongly in favor of the world. I've experienced an incredible love of the world, a lot of excitement and juice. During the second question, I saw more than I thought I would. But with the third one, I started comparing, and I said something like, "Love of the world is so much juicier—" And then I got these waves of presence and I couldn't say . . . it's like my mouth wouldn't say, "juicier than my love for spiritual freedom." And I started laughing. That felt like a lie, it felt like a complete betrayal of the truth I was experiencing in that moment. I experienced the truth of them being exactly the same, through the presence that was so intense in that moment. It felt like two magnets, pushing back and forth, and I felt like I was going to explode. The energy was so intense. I didn't expect that. And that is what I most love about spiritual freedom—when I see something new that I didn't expect. I'm a pretty happy guy at the moment.

Karen: That makes me happy, too. Beautiful. I can't help but wonder where the juice comes from . . .

Student: I had a beautiful experience with the questions. I hardly could split them up—love of the world and love of spiritual freedom. In the last question, it got clear that they are one unless I make a border—which I do now and then.

Several days ago, I was making music in the streets of Antwerp, streaming and flowing, and a man came to me and wanted to sing with me. It was beautiful to sing together. It was a giving and receiving at the same time. Later on, a student was there with her father, and they were taking pictures of us for a special project. We were all communicating with each other.

Afterward, I went to a restaurant, and as I was ordering my meal, I felt so open, really. I was there sitting, and anyone who came in I had contact with, through my eyes or a smile or something. A woman came in and was going to sit several tables further on, and we smiled—oh, you know what is coming . . . She ordered a beautiful pink drink—I don't know if you know what is coming . . . I wonder what you think is coming . . .

When my meal was served, she said, "Cheerio, have a good meal!" And then I noticed I was looking away, looking outside. I was thinking, "What is going to happen here?" I was losing my openness. I was making the boundary at that moment. It was so remarkable. I had felt so open until that moment, and then I thought, "What is she expecting from me? What is going to happen now?" Well, nothing was going to happen, of course. But that moment made it clear that this is all in me. It is all me who is separating things . . . and sometimes not. So, I'm happy.

Karen: So then what happened?

Student: I had a very good meal. It was very nice, and I was happy with the experience. Of course, I greeted the woman kindly when I left the restaurant. And that was it. Sorry to disappoint you.

Karen: It sounds like you were going with the openness and what was happening, and then you had to do something about it . . . create a boundary of some kind.

Student: I got afraid of what would happen if I am open.

Karen: So then a barrier comes. Thank you. Barriers and boundaries are part of our usual consciousness. It is the usual ego state to have inner and outer boundaries. These will be challenged by our work here. And perhaps some of them will melt through our understanding them.

Student: I noticed yesterday, but also today in my inquiry, that for me, love of the world and love of the spiritual have a lot to do with direction and flow. When I feel there is something flowing out of me and I feel full, then I feel they are the same—my desire and my love for the world and the place where the desire comes from are all one. I feel great, and my desire is a moving out to be close with whatever I desire. But there are also times when I feel like it is the other way around. Then I feel like a big black hole and that things need to come to me; I feel like a big mouth. Then I don't feel the love; I don't feel the love for the world and I don't feel the love for the spiritual. I am completely lost in that place—where are these two loves? It is mind-boggling that one of them feels so great and the other feels so awful.

Karen: We feel great when we are connected to something more real. We don't feel great when we lose it. That is when our practices are important. But it is also important to recognize that not all spiritual work is based on love for the spiritual. Some people enter into the spiritual through interest or suffering. And there are other reasons. In our work, love is the main fuel for the flame—actually, for enlightenment. And that love is a good and pleasurable feeling.

When that feeling is not there, our implicit love for the truth has to be present so we can stay with where we are. We can let ourselves feel like a hungry mouth, or feel like we are in hell—wherever that is—and continue to let that unfold and see what it's about. The disconnection is very painful, but that is when our love and our commitment to reality are tested the most.

Student: I did realize this morning that, in that place when I don't see at the moment that they are both present, somehow they both must be present there anyway and I just have to continue looking for them.

Karen: "Looking for them" might be one way of putting it. How I would put it is: Allow yourself to at least be interested in what the disconnect is. In fact, from my point of view, when we feel our love for the spiritual, it is the love for knowing what is there, what is happening in that moment. If I know what is disconnecting me, I learn something about myself that can potentially renew that connection. Not just by trying to look for the connection and then finding it and then pulling myself toward it again, but by actually finding out: What is this emptiness? this desolation? this pain? this suffering?

We need the love for the truth of where we are.

Love brings up all kinds of things that we need to understand. It helps us in our life when we understand what that hungry mouth is and whose it is, and why the pain and suffering are there. When I feel those things and let myself settle into that desperation and hunger and feel the truth of it, something comes to my aid unbidden. And it is a surprise, just like when the gentleman talked about being surprised by his love for the world and the spirit. It was a surprise in the way it emerged.

We don't always know what's going to answer the quest. This means letting yourself be a hungry mouth and finding out—love that experience of hunger, too, in some way. It is a matter of embracing our experience as it is, not just trying to find out what made us feel good. Usually, if we try to find out what that good feeling was and try to grasp it, it is a clenching that doesn't allow us to flow into the next, naturally arising experience. And part of life is that ebb and flow—there is pain and suffering; there are all kinds of things we learn from. We don't have to detach from any of it.

Student: I was also caught by surprise by a beautiful experience in the last inquiry. I was sitting in a lot of bodily pain and sensing those pains, that discomfort. And I just said, "I'm curious about this"—and wow, something happened. This great sweetness and flow of presence appeared and grew into a beautiful tree with branches that could uphold.

Karen: What happened to your pain?

Student: It is not in the foreground. I can sense it, I can look at it, be with it, but it's not appearing in the way it was. It is more diluted.

Karen: Sensing it doesn't erase it but puts it in perspective.

Student: Yes, and it is still bubbling.

Karen: So you are not just feeling good, you are bubbling.

Student: Yes.

Karen: So there is energy in it.

Student: A very bubbly sense.

Student: I have a friend who is a Diamond Approach teacher. When I was walking, I saw her with a number of your teachers in Amsterdam, and they thanked me for the work I am doing on sustainability. They said, "You are the empress of sustainability," and I couldn't take it in, because there was so much love coming from them. I still feel very emotional when I talk about it, because I really feel I am doing my spiritual thing in this world that expresses the connection between my spiritual freedom and the world, yet I still couldn't take in this big compliment from them.

Karen: Thank you, empress.

We often bridge the spiritual into the world by actions that we are taking to benefit others—by doing acts of kindness, by helping optimize the health in the world or of other people. This is a very worthy and noble thing. There is more to being in the world and having our spiritual freedom, and one of the things that you are bringing up—which is very important—is about knowing who you are and being able to be the presence of what you are as you are making those things happen in the world. That is another level of spiritual freedom, which means that you actually know yourself at every moment to be timeless and outside of the world, at the same time that you are completely present and completely within the world, making yourself a servant of that timelessness.

There are various levels of what we do in the world as service and this particular level of service is about being able to have both sides at once, regardless of what action we are taking at the moment—whether it is a noble effort or we are brushing our teeth. When the original goodness of consciousness is active and flowing through into the world, we become able to serve more from a place of selflessness. When the purity of our nature is obscured or we are in the midst of some difficulty, it is harder to do. So it is a process of growing into our natural condition, working through what keeps us from being a more open source of goodness. As we do that, we can integrate further; then our action comes more and more from clarity.

Probably many of you are taking many helpful actions, doing many good things, and that is to be honored. The next step is to actually *be* that presence that is fundamentally the active participant.

If we are not feeling authentic in our relationships, if we are not feeling real, we miss that. When we are feeling very present and very clear but are not able to engage personally, that's what we miss. So we want to bring the two sides together in such a way that we learn what giving and taking really are about.

Not being able to receive what those people said to you means that you don't know yet that you are worthy, that you are valued and valuable, that you are loved. Whether we are loved or not is always a big question: "Does this person like me? Does she not like me? Uh-oh, she *does* like me, so now what will she expect of me?" Or "She doesn't expect anything, so maybe she doesn't like me . . ." It goes around and around. A big one is: "I'm in love, but what if he doesn't love me?" Love is a big question for us.

The other side is, "I don't care whether she likes me—or whether he loves me—I'm involved in my intellectual pursuits." Or "I'm totally happy just with my spiritual life. That's what I love, that's all that interests me—the rest is just gravy." But this is a way of distancing from the issue of love. And as we are seeing, love is a central theme.

MUSIC MEDITATION

Suggested Selection:

"Adagio molto expressivo" from Beethoven's *Spring* Sonata (Violin Sonata No. 5 in F major, op. 24)

We end now with a music meditation on the very subject of love, because love is what brings things together. Love is what enables our barriers to melt—the boundaries inside of us that keep us divided, the boundaries between us that keep us separated from another or our own nature.

Love is the universal solvent. It is expressed through music, through song, through poetry, through many other creative pursuits; but nothing is as poignant or dissolving as the presence of love itself—the presence, the here-ness, the pooling, the collecting, the distillation, of what we call love.

In this meditation, we will make our mind work for our heart, through a visualization that will evoke the presence of love in us. If we suspend our notions and simply look into our heart and feel what is there, we will see that there is either a barrier against love or the ever-present flowing of it. Wherever you are with that, just allow your experience as you listen to the music.

We recommend that you listen to the second movement ("Adagio molto expressivo") of Beethoven's *Spring* Sonata if it is available. If it is not, choose a piece of music that you know tends to evoke the experience, the presence, of love in you; it just needs to be a type of music that you think will provide a space for that opening. After you put the music on, and are settled comfortably, start the exercise by visualizing a golden liquid dribbling down on you and descending into your head. From there, see it melting and collecting in a golden chalice in your chest. This golden fluid that is filling your chest now is sweet, rich, nourishing. It feels soft and full and sweet, like honey but not sticky.

As this is happening, allow yourself to breathe into your belly. Be present in your belly. Developing the belly center will make the experience of this meditation more than just visual; you will actually sense and feel this subtle substance from inside yourself.

As you continue to listen to the music, allow yourself to feel that fluid substance descending as you visualize it. If you can't visualize it, simply sit and feel your belly. Just let your experience open up to it.

After the musical selection is finished, sit for a few minutes in silence.

3

Two Worlds

HAMEED

W E WILL BEGIN WITH A CHANT, which you will do sitting in an upright and settled position as if you were meditating. We will chant the word HU, which is taken by many Sufis to be the secret name of the Divine, the ultimate nature of everybody and everything. Take a breath and make the sound on a long, sustained exhalation—*hoooo*. When you finish exhaling, take another breath and repeat the sound—and continue doing this over and over. You want to simply allow the sound to come out of you, not to push or force it.

Chanting HU is an invitation to our deeper nature, our source, to manifest and speak through us in whatever way it chooses. The sound you make can be loud or soft, and on whatever pitch is comfortable for your voice. It is recommended that you do this chant for ten or fifteen minutes. After you stop the chant, continue sitting in silence, practicing the belly meditation for another ten or fifteen minutes.

FINDING THE INVISIBLE WORLD

There is a Zen saying that describes the primary stages of the path: "First there is a mountain, then there is no mountain, then there is a mountain." The second mountain is very different from the first mountain, however, because we have traveled the whole path. It is the same mountain, yet we experience it, and the whole of realty, in a totally new way.

Zen practitioners do things such as koan practice and zazen, sitting meditation. Although we engage in meditations of various kinds, our main practice in the Diamond Approach is inquiry into ordinary experience. When we inquire into our ordinary experience, we see that it contains things that are of the first mountain. Ordinary experience says that there is a mountain, there is me, there is you, there is the world. And all of this is seen from the ordinary perspective: There is this mountain and that other mountain—all these mountains, just as there are all these people and all these things. Everything is actually seen from an isolated, mental perspective, a perspective that views reality as being composed of many things. And we tend to see this many-ness of things in terms of divisions and polarities.

Exploring the divisions within our experience and understanding how they become separated into opposing sectors can be a rich inquiry. Understanding the opposition, the conflict, and the polarity will resolve to an underlying truth, which is the second mountain. But in the process, dissolution occurs. There is loss, there is annihilation of whatever it is we are exploring—and that is true about anything we explore in our personal experience. This is the state of no mountain. If we fully explore any of our experiences, any of the objects of our experience, any of the content of our experience, in order to understand it as completely as possible, at some point the process will reveal things that we don't see at the beginning. The process begins to reveal the invisible world, the world that we don't see with our senses, with our ordinary eyes. This will feel like a loss, but through the loss a discovery is uncovered.

THE DIVISION AND POLARITY IN LOVING

We have been working with the division between wanting (or desire) and selfless love, which eros will unify if we truly understand what eros is. We say that Eros is the god of sexual love or desire. But what is sexual love, what is erotic love? That is why we use the term "divine eros" here—so that we can reveal the meaning of eros as we are discussing it. We have worked with the polarity of the two loves and examined how our heart is divided: We love the world, we care for the world, we care for everything in the world—for the earth, for the people in it, for the life in the world. If we explore that caring, that interest, we begin to recognize the very powerful love that we have for the world, a love that many people don't recognize until they are about to die.

People who are near death sometimes begin to see how much they love life, how much they love the world, how much they love very simple things. To be able to get up and take a shower is wonderful. You don't want to lose that . . . just feeling the water running over your body. Normally, you don't tend to notice that; you just take a shower every morning and put on your clothes and run. But when you are about to die, you think, "Oh, am I never going to have a shower again?" and you recognize how much you like it, how much you love it.

If we explore our relationship to the world, we recognize that we have a tremendous love for it. We have a deep love for the world even though many of us have difficulty with it. We have fears and conflicts about the world, and there is much suffering, pain, aggression, and disappointment. Some of us sometimes hate the world. But when we explore very deeply, we usually recognize that we feel love for it as well. At the same time, we have another love. Many people in the world are not aware of this other love. They are only living out their love, their attraction to and their need for the world. But when somebody becomes more mature or sensitive, the conventional world is no longer enough. The life of the world, regardless of how much we love it, feels incomplete at some point. Every aspect of it, regardless of how beautiful, how wonderful, it is, has something about it that is not completely satisfying. Even with people we love, in our intimate love relationships, and in our connection with nature, we hunger for something else, something more invisible. We can't even define at first what that is.

We become aware of this love in different ways. Some of us feel discontented, incomplete, or we become aware of a sense of meaninglessness. Some of us have a lot of pain and suffering and want to end that; so we seek happiness or freedom. That is why many spiritual teachings see as the motivation for enlightenment and spirituality the need to develop compassion, or to free people from suffering, or to have love for God or for truth. But if we explore all of these, we begin to recognize this other love, the love for what is beyond this world. Anyone who becomes interested in inner work, spiritual work, starts to be aware of this love.

Many spiritual teachings say, "Let's forget about the world. The world will not bring freedom, won't bring true fulfillment. Let's move deeper or higher; let's go into the other world." That perspective points to the value of spiritual work, spiritual realization and enlightenment. Yet it is one-sided, dividing world from spirit.

It is the nature of spiritual experience and realization that we feel we are disengaging from the world. The deeper we go into the spiritual ground, the more we feel we are losing things in the world. And we assume that we have to let go of our attachments. We think we need to release our attachment to our bodies, to other people's bodies. We have to let go of our attachments to our cars, our homes, our mobile phones—all the things we love and enjoy. We feel that we have to give up many things we love, and many spiritual traditions support that: "Yes, you have to surrender these things; they should not be that important to you. The spiritual, God, buddha nature—these are what bring true freedom, true happiness." Many people who manage to experience the vastness, the depth, the infinity, the eternity of our nature and its miraculousness and mystery, can feel at some point that the world and everything in it is not important.

You might have experiences that the world is all gone—this is the stage of no mountain. However—and frequently—the first love reasserts itself because the spiritual dimension does not seem complete on its own. The spiritual, whether we think of it as God or not, is not complete without the world. (This ties in with theories of why God created the world. Some teachings take the position that God was alone, lonely, and wanted a consort. By creating the world, he would be more complete.)

Many teachings say not to care about the world. Some say that enjoyment of the world, particularly the enjoyment of the body, is sinful, is bad, because it takes us away from the divine. For these traditions, "divine" means forgetting about the world; we just want God, we only want the inner Beloved—only the truth, only realization. But if we move exclusively toward the spiritual and think, "Let's renounce the world and let go of everything," we end up with half of real life. The extreme expression of that is to go into a monastery and forget about the world. On the other hand, if we emphasize the world and our relationships in it at the expense of spiritual depth, spiritual truth, then after a while even the most beautiful intimate relationship begins to be empty and meaningless and will create more suffering.

In fact, as we move through the inner journey, we feel a pull, a movement, a love, toward the spiritual pole, which makes us feel that we are going away from the world and from the people in the world. This will bring up our attachment and, underlying that, the love of the world and beings of the world and things of the world.

But, again, just to be in the spiritual and forget the world will feel to most people not completely satisfying, regardless of how blissful their spiritual experience. Even the experience of the spiritual ground—when we get to our spiritual home and are living in that intimacy—is beautiful, but at some point, it feels like something is not right, not complete. And we begin to be aware that "Yes, I love the spirit—but I also love the world." Whenever we emphasize one part at the expense of the other, we begin to feel a state of incompleteness.

Many of us do a lot of things to attempt to bring the two

together, to harmonize the two loves. And some of you have seen how, when you really feel the love, it is not two loves. But our heart is divided mainly because of our mind. Our mind believes that there are two worlds, two realities. One is the physical world—the everyday world of me, you, everybody else; the houses, cars, planets, and galaxies. The other is the world of spirit, the world of mystery—the unseen, invisible world, the world of total harmony, the world of purity, of pure light, pure radiance, perfect presence, the world of the divine.

For a long time throughout the inner journey, we tend to think that there are two kinds of experience, as if there were two realities, two worlds. Even when we have a spiritual experience, we imagine that it came from somewhere else, from the "other world," from spirit, or from the spiritual dimension. So there is a division in our mind, a duality. We believe in a duality between the world and the spirit, between matter and spirit, between the body and spiritual nature. This is a deeply held belief, very profound. It is not a matter of conscious, mental conviction. You may study and believe in the teachings of nonduality, but the way you are in the world will exemplify your actual underlying convictions.

Every thought we think, every feeling we feel, every action we take implies the position we hold about this world and the ways we perceive it. For most people, nothing else exists beyond the visible; there is only this world, and you try to survive and make the best of it. Those who are involved in spiritual practice usually think there is more than what appears to us as physical reality. Regardless of what we believe, including our notions of nonduality or unity, we still think and behave as if there were two worlds. And this belief splits our heart in two, so that we end up with two loves. We love the world, but we also love spiritual freedom—we love the spirit and its harmony, its blissfulness, its sanctity, its majesty and beauty.

One Reality

This situation shows us how the second mountain is different from the first mountain. The second mountain is the same mountain as the first, but is seen without the dualistic point of view. When we see the second mountain, our heart is unified. We don't have two loves. We have only one love—because there is only one reality. This points again to the juxtaposition of the two terms "divine" and "eros." The first represents the spiritual world and the second represents this world, but divine eros combines them. When we see their reality, we recognize that they are inseparable. They are not only inseparable, they are one. When we see the spirit completely for what it is, we know that what is called the spiritual universe is nothing but the true underlying condition of this world.

It is not only that there is a spiritual world parallel to the physical world. It is not only a question of parallel universes or two worlds that sometimes cross in our experience. There is ultimately only one. They are actually never separate; they seem separate only because our mind sees them that way. And because our mind sees them as separate, we have two loves. But at the very depth of our heart, we love reality. We love the real, and the real is the unity of the outer and the inner, of your body and your soul, of the world and God, of the ordinary universe and the spiritual universe. These are like the front and the back of the same reality. This world is nothing but the front of reality. The spirit is the back of this reality. And you can't take the back away from the front. It doesn't work, for the front will always have a back, which is the spiritual nature.

One interesting thing about what we call reality is the distance between the back and the front. How big is this distance? Many of us say, "Oh, it's far; it takes a lot of work to get there, it takes a long time to travel there." We refer to taking a journey, traveling, flying. And even moving at the speed of light, it takes years for many people. But when you recognize the second mountain and why it is said, ". . . and then there is a mountain," this is all that needs to be said, because the distance between spirit—that luminosity, that purity, that absolute brilliant clarity—and your body and the visible world is zero. There is no distance whatsoever—never has been a distance, never will be a distance. There can't be. That would be like saying that there is a distance between your atoms and your skin. What is the distance between your skin and its atoms? Can you say? There is none, and it is not possible to even speak of the concept of distance, because the atoms are the nature of your skin; they are what make your skin.

So the spirit is what makes your body, it is what makes this world, it is what constitutes everything. That is why we call it true nature. It is the true nature of this world. It is my true nature, your true nature, the true nature of this building we are in. When we see the world and its true nature, when we see that the outer and the inner are simply the front and the back—completely inseparable, no distance between them—then we realize how amazingly, exquisitely radiant it all is. Everything that you see—the physical bodies present, the clothes people are wearing, the walls and the ceiling—begins to glitter and to shine with an inner radiance. All of it becomes self-illuminating jewels—jewels of light that are, at the same time, beauty and love and tenderness and consciousness. But we normally don't see it that way because we have this deep belief in separation.

When people consider the question, "What is the nature of the body?" they mostly think of atoms or elementary particles. If they are more sophisticated, they may think of strings or quarks. But whether you think in terms of atomic theory or string theory, your perspective is from the same dimension. There is another dimension that intersects all points of the universe; when we recognize it, it changes our perception of the entire world and all of reality.

Let's say you have a spiritual experience, such as a vision or an illumination, a manifestation of beautiful light or an experience of deep love—or maybe your heart becomes vast like space, full of compassion. These are only glimpses, little penetrations of the true light coming through your beliefs and penetrating the ideas and the concepts of your mind, giving you a peek at reality. And you believe that something new is occurring. That is how we think about it: "Something happened that has never happened before!" What we don't know is that when we opened the window, we opened to experience the light that is always there. So the true perspective is that we opened a little window and looked, and we saw the light—"Oh, it's brilliant, beautiful, intoxicating, pleasurable"—but actually nothing new happened. It's just that our perception changed.

Even so, we are afraid to open the window completely and leave it open, because it will mean not only that the "I" disappears—it means the whole world will disappear. And we don't want it to disappear, because we love it; we are totally in love with it.

We don't understand that we won't lose it. Why won't we lose it? Because this love we feel is the same as the love of no mountain. We don't see that it is the love of looking through the window and seeing empty space—beautiful, totally peaceful . . . nothing has happened, nothing ever happens—yet completely silent, no disturbance whatsoever—like before the Big Bang. But if you stay a little longer and keep looking, letting your love guide you, letting your heart guide you, you will see at some point that the silence—that quiet, peaceful luminosity, the space before the Big Bang—is still here. It hasn't disappeared. We simply were too busy with the material outcome of the Big Bang. We got occupied with all that was created. Our senses became focused on all of the things of the world, and we forgot to look at what is within them, within the space where all the activity happens.

Spirituality, at least in the Diamond Approach, means recognizing the true condition of reality and understanding through experience that it is much more mysterious than we think. The true condition of reality is that the physical and the spiritual are the same thing, yet this does not mean they are identical. The mountain comes back again. It is the same mountain; nothing changes in it, yet it has become God's appearance. Look at the mountain—you don't see the burning bush, you just see God. That mountain is God . . . but it is also the mountain. Which one do you love? You don't have to decide, because they are the same.

You will experience conflict or disharmony between the two if you divide God and the mountain into two separate things. To want only one is to want an impossibility, because one doesn't exist without the other. If you only want the world, that is not possible. If you only want spirit, that is not possible. You can't help but want both, because the two are the same thing—a unity that we can experience in various ways, depending on our level of spiritual realization. Thus, when you separate that which is the same, you experience conflict, because deep inside of you is unity, and what you have divided into two is actually the same thing. You are the spirit. Who else do you think is looking at me? If you are not the spirit, you will not hear, you will not see, you will have no sensitivity.

The more we see the true nature of reality, the more we recognize that the division in our heart is a by-product of our own belief, our own position about reality. However, our heart is primordially, originally, timelessly, and eternally undivided. So perhaps you are beginning to understand what we mean by "divine eros." When you love another person, you also want him or her—but what is it that you love and what is it that you want? Their body? Yes or no? Yes, but not only. If it's just the body, that would mean wanting an empty shell. If you only want their spirit, there would be no possibility of complete relating on this level of existence that we are living this moment. You need both, and that is what brings about true divine eros. So, what does "eros" mean? And why do we say that eros is divine? Because it forcefully divulges the true nature of love.

If you really love, you see the whole picture. If you truly love somebody, you see that he or she is not different from the divine. So when you love this person, you love the divine—if the love is complete. And if you love the divine, you don't love only one person; you love everything and everybody, because the divine comes through everything and everybody. So, as you begin to recognize the divine coming through all forms, all bodies, and all manifestations, your perception changes. It is the same mountain and, at the same time, it is transparent. It is as though you could see through the rocks, through the trees. It is not that you see objects behind other objects because things are physically transparent; that is not what we mean. You are able to see through everything, to the center of the universe, to the essence of it. You look at the mountain and into the mountain, and it opens into inner space and pure light, but it is still the mountain.

With this background, we can now discuss how our new understanding impacts relationships: When we see from this perspective, what happens to our relationship to the world, to our relationships with other human beings, including sexual relationships?

LIVING IN REALITY

Eros is a god, and the true mission of eros is to bring us to the experience and realization of what real love can be in all its dimensions. Eros shows us how love unifies not only spirit and body, but also desire with selfless giving. In wanting your partner, lover, husband or wife, you are giving them your heart. But this is not the kind of wanting that most people know. When we feel wanting and desire, we experience it at the level of the first mountain, which most people call eros. But in our exploration, we want to know the true nature of divine eros, which is the same as seeing it from the perspective of the second mountain.

The two sides, the front and the back, are both manifestations of the same truth, the same reality. It is possible, it is part of our potential, to have this unity, which means experiencing spiritual realization, experiencing our spiritual presence, in the particular situations of life, love, and love relationships. It means being aware of our inner spiritual purity and luminosity, aware of this radiant presence, at the same time that we are living our life, as we are walking, showering, interacting. Wouldn't you love that? You don't want to just have realization when you are meditating, or once in a while. It would be nice to have that awareness no matter what you are doing; then spirituality would not be a separate compartment of life. But most people think of spirituality in a compartmentalized way: "I have my work life, I have my family life, and I have my spiritual life."

Ideally, spiritual life is all of our life. Nothing is excluded. If something is excluded, that means we are misunderstanding what spiritual life is. Spiritual life is not just going to church, not just meditating, not just having some wonderful inner experiences. It is living in reality—being what we truly are and living in the world as it is. This is possible for us. It is our potential. Of course we want to recognize the spiritual world, but the greater potential is to recognize that the spiritual world is not separate from this physical world. The spiritual world is the light of this world, the true nature of this world, the true existence of this world—which means that it is your true existence. When you experience yourself right now, when you feel yourself right now—if you feel yourself completely—you will feel yourself as wonderful, amazing, a luminous presence.

If you are not feeling that, there are barriers inside, tensions and beliefs and ideas and obstacles in your perception, in your consciousness, and these obscurations are allowing reality to reach you only in the conventional way. Our fixed positions limit reality to the world as we normally know it.

We will do an exercise now to explore this situation, to inquire into how we tend to see reality as two worlds—as body and soul, matter and spirit, world and God, worldly life and spiritual life—and how these cannot be separated. If there is any hope for our world, it is in seeing that they are actually not separate.

EXPLORATION SESSION

Spend fifteen minutes in an investigation into the truth of how you experience the relationship between the physical world and the spiritual world. From the perspective of wanting to be inspired by eros, what can you see about how your mind perceives these worlds? What underlying conviction and position do you hold about the way you experience the relationship between the two?

In this investigation, you want to look at your experience and recognize the duality in it. Having had nondual teaching does not mean that duality has ended for you; you might believe in the nondual, but you are most likely still deeply convinced of duality. Some of your experience may even be nondual, but most of the time, and for most people, it is dualistic: me and my spirit, me and presence, me and you—all of these are dualities. By exploring how you experience things, you want to uncover your conviction of duality by identifying the underlying belief that makes you see things that way. What is your fundamental position? You want to see if you can find that.

QUESTIONS AND COMMENTS

Student: During exploration, I was angry and I felt that I needed a slice of bread. It started with the conflict that I shouldn't be eating something when I do a spiritual exercise, so the duality was immediately there. The more I tasted my slice of bread, the more I saw all kinds of duality that I believe in. It happened that when the slice of bread was gone, or a piece of it was in my belly, I didn't feel anything. Which meant that, in the end, I felt I was not, but the bread was chewed. I wasn't chewing it. My body wasn't there. It was totally transparent. It was so strange to be so intimate with the bread that my body vanished, totally vanished. Then I looked at my exercise partners and I heard their voices. I felt totally transparent; everything was so intimate with me . . . everybody.

Hameed: I get it . . . for you to be intimate with other people, your body had to disappear.

Student: Yet it was not my usual body anymore; it was totally peaceful, totally clear, totally natural.

Hameed: That is what we are: clear, peaceful, and natural. When we are truly ourselves, that is how it is.

Student: I wonder whether this is what you meant by "the second mountain." I was dealing with all these dichotomies, and then the slice of bread that I was chewing on . . . and then the slice of bread is chewed on. Then the mountain. All these pictures of me are gone—and suddenly that whole reality is one mountain for me. I am transparent.

Hameed: That is what happens. When you become transparent, there is only one reality, not many. It is a very good perception to realize how reality is. When we are truly ourselves, and completely transparent, everything becomes one thing, an indivisible reality.

Student: It is so sobering.

Hameed: The sobriety is a good sign because it means you are clear about the situation, recognizing things, seeing the truth instead of just being excited about it. You are seeing it, and it makes you sober. It wakes you up. That is why we call it awakening—you wake up to how things are. It's an interesting thing. It feels as if your body is disappearing, even though it is chewing the bread. When you become one with the piece of bread, you are transparent and the bread is transparent. And you have become one with it in more than one way—it's both physical and nonphysical. So life can be very interesting that way. Just see how it can be: You could be riding your bicycle later and wonder who is riding. The bicycle will be ridden, in the same way as you said, "The bread is being chewed."

Student: I shared a time, which has often come back to me, when I had a sense of oneness. During the feedback, my exercise partners had to remind me of that sense of oneness. After they pointed it out, I noticed as I was walking down the stairs during the break that my wonderful superego—or in my case, the inner committee—immediately started to evaluate it. It started to say, "What you were talking about . . . is it good enough?" Once again, this ego of mine doesn't want to acknowledge this oneness and this unity. It wants to pull me back into duality.

Hameed: Of course.

Student: It really pisses me off.

Hameed: I'm glad it pisses you off—that's good. So when you get pissed off, right now, what happens? How do you experience yourself? You recognize that you are pissed off about this committee trying to evaluate your experience. Obliterate the committee, and what will be left?

Student: That is the problem. If the inner committee goes, there is nothing left of the ego.

Hameed: What is left now that you are pissed at the committee?

Student: Fear. I don't like to trust my gut instincts.

Hameed: It is important to recognize that fear is there. Maybe this is what brings back the committee—to protect you from that fear. The committee believes it is protecting you.

Student: That's right . . . because if I trust, I have to step off a cliff, believe my gut instinct—and I don't know whether I am going to fall or fly.

Hameed: Are you sure there will be any difference—fall or fly?

Student: Because if I fall will you be there to catch me?

Hameed: Remember what was just said: Everything is transparent. But there is the fear that we are going to fall; we are going to step off that cliff and fall, and nothing will hold us. That is really terrifying for us. So our conviction of that duality makes us very scared, and the fear is very real. This shows how deep our conviction is and how much we believe in duality. What are you experiencing now?

Student: More courage than I normally have—courage is usually not one of my stronger suits. There is a sense that even if I fall, I have more lives to live . . . so go ahead and try it.

Hameed: You are feeling more boldness, more courage?

Student: Yes.

Hameed: You want to be more adventurous?

Student: Let's not go too far.

Hameed: I thought I was taking a step at a time.

Student: Baby steps, please.

Hameed: Very good . . . I listen. One step at a time for all of us, because when we feel those fears, they are really strong. They control our experience in a big way. Even though, in reality, there is nothing to be afraid of about stepping off that cliff, we still have much fear. As a result, there's a lot of conflict and difficulty and, as you said, committees deliberating what is real and what is not real, what is good and what is not good.

Many teachings do not deal with this dimension of difficulties; they use yogic techniques of concentration, prayer, or even philosophy to get to the second mountain, without going through these difficulties. But the problems will remain and will resurface during the course of daily life. Therefore, in the Diamond Approach, we deal with such difficulties in ordinary experience, and these actually become doorways to the second mountain.

Student: My experience was along the same line, except in my case, it concerns the boundary, the physical body. I need a lot of assurance. It took me courage to stand up and speak. I figured that I need to find out what this pain in my shoulder is all about. And I noticed that I was squeezing it so hard so that I can support myself. It is like I was trying to support the whole world. I started laughing: "This is ridiculous, this doesn't work."

Hameed: Very good point. Trying to hold on to your body so that you don't lose it is sort of ridiculous.

Student: It doesn't work.

Hameed: The body is there anyway, whether you hold on to it or not.

Student: It is more like holding on for life—that is how it feels.

Hameed: I know. You hold on for dear life. It is deeply instinctual. It is an animal instinct to hold on in order to keep your body and your world from disappearing. But remember the Zen saying: First there is a mountain, and then there is no mountain, then there is a mountain. "No mountain" is a stage. Hearing this might give you a little bit of comfort, but it is usually not enough. You have to feel the fear. But it is okay to feel the fear, to embrace it, because here we inquire into everything, all of our ordinary experience. And it is part of our normal experience to feel that kind of fear, the fear of losing the boundaries.

Student: It is so alone, feels so alone.

Hameed: You are going to be alone?

Student: A tiny bit of hope is there, and it feels familiar.

Hameed: When you feel so alone—not thinking it is a bad thing or a good thing but just feeling it—what's it like? If you don't judge it as good or bad, and whether it should end or not—if you don't have an opinion about it— what do you discover about that alone place?

Student: It is very still.

Hameed: So, that alone place has stillness in it.

Student: Nothing moves.

Hameed: It is still . . . nothing moves. So you see, first you were saying that it is alone, and you were thinking that this is a bad thing; but now when you don't judge it, you realize it is really very still; nothing moves. How is it for you when it feels still like that?

Student: It makes me think of a dead body.

Hameed: Okay, it doesn't move, and that means it is a dead body. Interesting . . . a dead body talking. That is a very interesting paradox, and paradox is important. But if you continue feeling the stillness—just the stillness itself, the alone stillness, without thinking whether it is your body, either alive or dead—what's it like?

Student: It is just everywhere.

Hameed: Stillness is everywhere, right. And when you feel that it is everywhere, what does that make you feel?

Student: It is a sense of awe.

Hameed: Everywhere is still, just like that. That is how it really is—everywhere. So, surprise, huh? It starts with the fear of letting go of your boundaries, fear that you are going to lose your body. Then you feel alone. As you explore that and let it happen, it becomes a stillness. Then you associate stillness with death, with your body. When you let go of that and keep exploring, you realize, "Oh, it is everywhere." That is awesome.

Student: I still don't feel comfortable with it.

Hameed: Of course you don't feel comfortable with it now. What is uncomfortable about it?

Student: I feel like I'm fixed, frozen. Stuck in the stillness.

Hameed: If you feel stuck in it that means you think stillness is a bad thing. If you don't think of it as good or bad, if you don't judge it but just explore it, what do you find?

Student: That you are talking.

Hameed: That's interesting. There is stillness here, but I'm talking. You are talking too, right? That means your mind thinks of stillness as stuckness. First you thought of it as death, and now you are thinking of it as stuckness, but the stillness, as you see, does not mean that there is no movement. It is a paradox.

How is the discomfort now? When you see that stillness is everywhere, there is awe. Is there anything else about the stillness that you can tell me besides its being still? What is the feeling of the stillness?

Student: It is empty.

Hameed: Still and empty. Is that what makes you more uncomfortable?

Student: Yes.

Hameed: I thought so. It is not only still, it is empty. What is the association with empty?

Student: I can't believe I am standing up.

Hameed: You can't believe you are standing up. You are standing up, you are talking, but it is still and empty at the same time. Do you feel the stillness inside you? No? You just see it everywhere but not inside you?

Student: I notice that the chronic pain I used to have in the chest is gone, surprisingly.

Hameed: So that is one side effect of empty stillness.

Student: It's gone. From here down, it is okay, it is just fine, it is kosher. And from here to here, it is not kosher.

Hameed: Not kosher because it is empty here . . . what do you mean "not kosher"?

Student: It is like it is saying, "Close your eyes."

Hameed: Aha, yeah . . .

Student: It says, "Don't look."

Hameed: It says, "Don't look." What happens when you close your eyes? Try it and see.

Student: Nothing happens . . . but there is something here.

Hameed: The experience keeps developing; different things happen. Is the discomfort more or less now?

Student: Same.

Hameed: The discomfort might come and go, but it would be interesting to find out what the discomfort is: Is it fear or is it something else? Are you not believing what you are experiencing?

Student: I'm not believing it.

Hameed: You don't believe it. Yes, reality is difficult to understand. That's what happens when we see that the spirit is the back of reality. Reality is always in motion, always in movement; a lot is happening, but reality, the spirit part, is very still. It is just like deep space. And the two are completely inseparable, which is why you can talk while you are still.

Student: The stillness is just beginning to come inside.

Hameed: It is difficult to believe because it doesn't make sense to our mind. This shows that the perception of nonduality has many things in it, very profound things that don't make sense, such as movement and stillness at the same time. How can that be? Nonduality means that they are the same. You and I are the same. Stillness is everywhere. Something and nothing are the same. Everybody is here, but the stillness feels like nothing.

As we are seeing, there is more to reality than meets the eye. Even the ordinary world can be seen in a very different way that doesn't make sense to our mind. It is important at such times to pay some attention to our fears, our conflicts, our beliefs and ideas about things in the world, the things we don't believe . . . and our feelings about all of that.

––––––––––––

Student: There is a video on YouTube about a woman who experienced a hemorrhage; Jill Bolte Taylor is her name. She begins by describing the brain and how it consists of two separate parts. She'd had a hemorrhage, and as the blood was gushing in her left part of her brain, she was experiencing oneness with everything. She describes how she was looking at her arm and could see that it was the same as everything around her, so she could feel one with everything, experiencing the light and happiness inside of her.

Hameed: I think I've seen the video, but thanks for mentioning it so that other people can see it. She is a scientist. So what does it make you feel to have seen that?

Student: I have been following a Sufi path for a number of years, and it involves looking for guidance in somebody else who can lead you—a master who can bring you to God, to the divine, to the spirit, as a representative of God. So the video had me wondering whether the trip from me to God is one and a half centimeters long in my mind but I just don't know how to make the switch. And the movement between first mountain and second mountain is in the same space—they are just a short distance away from each other—and I don't know how to discover it. And if the master came up with a set of exercises and rules to guide me . . . maybe there are other ways of making the transition.

Hameed: I think there are other ways besides having a hemorrhage.

Student: Definitely! I don't think I would like to experience that in order to have the experience of oneness.

Hameed: But there are many kinds of hemorrhages: emotional hemorrhage, mental hemorrhage . . . that is what happens when the idea of the self begins to soften up and melt. It is really a kind of hemorrhage, because our concept of the self gets softer and mushier and begins to disappear; it doesn't work the way it usually does. You may have a very interesting experience at such a time. But we are working here in a way that makes it unnecessary to wait for that special moment for something to happen. We only need to work with our ordinary, everyday experience, whatever we are experiencing—our thoughts, our feelings, our beliefs. If we stay with that, remain present with it, embrace it and understand it as much as we can, our experience will reveal unity, nonduality, because that is the underlying truth of all of our experiences.

Next, we will see what eros has to say about stillness.

4

One Desire

KAREN

A S WE CONTINUE TO EXPLORE, we will come to understand that part of our practice is to become aware of the way we deal with the openings that arise along the journey. For example, in our encounters with new dimensions of our experience, certain energies become liberated, and it is important that we don't act on them right away. All kinds of feelings can be stimulated that will not yet be completely understood, and if we attempt to make decisions and take action prematurely, we might create more difficulties for ourselves or others. What we want is to be able to feel what is true, without our feelings automatically discharging through the filters of our mind, heart, and body in habitual ways. Otherwise, we are using the potential of our nature in a way that does not assist its evolution into a new realm of experience; instead, our usual patterns continue, with even more force.

In addition, discharging the energies that arise tends to dilute their impact. So it is helpful to contain whatever is arising in your experience, not by holding back any feelings but by feeling them fully without acting on them. As we continue in our process, I invite you to feel as deeply as you can everything that comes forward, regardless of what it is. Allow it to come up, and really feel it, sense it, be with it—stay with it—and let it open up. This is important because we are going to be exploring more deeply various areas in our consciousness that perhaps have held a lot of charge for you. Opening to these places will mean going beyond the repression of our typical ego defenses, and this can bring out a great deal of energy and the tendency to want to do something with it. We are venturing into an area that is challenging, both conceptually and experientially.

So when we engage in a practice that enables our consciousness to expand, we need to be aware not to feed our habitual responses and reactions. This intention and attitude is important to embrace as an ongoing part of practice.

As you find yourself experiencing new qualities and forms of consciousness, it is important to allow them to transform you, instead of the ego getting fortified. For if you express what comes forward automatically and impulsively, what you will end up with is simply a bigger, new-and-improved ego self. We are always faced with these two possibilities: Depending on how we approach our awakening to new realms, we can either expand our ego self or be transformed to express a whole new level of existence. Transformation requires that we learn how to meet and invite this alchemical process through being with and understanding experience. This will allow it to express its own intelligent unfolding.

In this territory we are exploring, we learn that love has more dimensions to it than we usually consider. We have already started to discuss some ways that love is more than the love we have known thus far—for example, that it is a presence with a textured, appealing quality. Emotionally, we can intuit that love is sweet and soft, but the more directly and immediately we feel and know that love, the more we are in touch with its palpable, textured reality. Then we are able to see that the essence of love is divine. However, because eros amplifies the force implicit in this love, it can bring up a lot of unconscious content for people. Many of you are already becoming aware of the ways that your ideas, thoughts, and conditioning have colored your feelings about love as well as about eros. Clarifying these, seeing through them, and understanding more clearly our relationship to love and eros will bring in more palpably the presence of love with the energetic power of eros. This will impact you in various ways. The expansion that results from going beyond your usual view and experience of love and the potent force of eros may bring a sense of liberation of heart energy or may rattle some of you a bit. But this will give you the opportunity to see the ways that your consciousness has been limited. Then, over time, as you understand that you are this liberated consciousness, you can learn to act from a new and freshly invigorated place.

Freeing Desire from the Past

Questioning your attitudes about love is a powerful exploration in and of itself, but bringing attention to the element that unveils the erotic and infuses love with erotic energy is a further challenge to your sense of reality and the self that lives that ordinary reality. That element is desire.

When you consider the word "desire," what goes on in your belly? What sensations do you feel in your body? What do you feel in your heart? Also notice what happens in your mind—what associations are you having? Take a minute now to sense the totality of your experience.

The thought of desire can produce many feelings, both pleasurable and not so pleasurable: anxiety, intrigue, disgust, anticipation, excitement, and so on. Some of you may be thinking, "Oh good, I get to feel desire; I don't usually have that opportunity." Others may be thinking, "Uh-oh, my desire might get out of control, and that can get dangerous." Some of you may be afraid of disappearing or losing yourselves in your desire. On the other hand, need and dependency are often associated with desire, and they tend to stimulate a different set of reactions: "Oh my God, somebody is going to see my neediness, my wanting—and then what? It'll be too much . . . my desire is too big . . . it's huge . . . it's as big as the universe. If somebody sees it, I'm going to get rejected . . . Or worse yet, I'm going to eat *them* up or something terrible is going to happen."

Each individual has his or her unique story about desire and what prohibits fully experiencing it, but we all feel desire to some degree. Under the usual constraints of ego structure, however, our experience of desire is limited. We have all heard many admonitions against it: Desire needs to be under control. Desire could lead to bad behavior; it can make us do things we shouldn't do. Desire shouldn't be shown too much; it is socially unacceptable. Desire is scary or embarrassing. Desire is childish and immature. Some of us may even think, "I don't feel desire. I don't even feel a desire to feel de- sire." As you explore what is true for you about this, do not strive to have a "correct" experience of desire; don't try to shape your desire in any way. You simply want to become aware of the relationship that you currently have with it.

Desire is a natural force in us; it's a natural condition. In the same way that love is a natural condition, desire is also natural. We have reactions, ideas, and beliefs about desire because some- where within our consciousness we *know* it. Desire existed within our psyche long before we had a sense of who was desiring anything. It is more fundamental than who we have come to know ourselves to be.

Eros is more than desire, but desire is an important expression of it. We can relate to desire in many different ways, but without desire, eros is dead. On the other hand, bringing the desire element into our love creates the feeling of erotic love, that robust feeling of juiciness that we enjoy and want. We may desire our desire to come forward when we see how it interfaces with love.

Desire can be seen in any baby. Desire can be seen in children. Children let themselves passionately want what they want—at times, they scream and yell and have a tantrum about it. As we get older, we become a little more sophisticated; we scream and yell in- ternally about what we want. We learn that we can't always have what we want exactly the way we want it, so we end up interfering with our experience in order to handle the painful condition of not having our needs and desires responded to. The natural force of our wanting gets dimmer; that energetic surge is muffled. Our desire as adults tends to get focused on useful things: career, appliances, social or political action, for example.

At some point, we may start to have a craving of the kind we have been describing here—for something more or deeper that we can't name. And perhaps our desire wants to express itself in a new way but we can't seem to allow that force to take us toward what we want. We are blocked by our ideas of what desire has meant to us in the past. In fact, initially, we may not even recognize the force in us as desire.

Most of us think of desire as being always for something outside us, so it is difficult to imagine desire without it being focused on an object. Take the situation of falling in love. As long as our experience of desire is attached to another person or situation, we believe that love itself is dependent on the outside. Unless our love is liberated from this attachment, our full potential to love—which is present in us whether we are relating to another person or not—cannot reveal itself to us. But we will never reach that freedom unless we first allow ourselves to completely feel our wanting as it is. And the ego has a hard time doing that.

When we first fall in love, the door opens and the barriers to desire loosen their grip. We experience ourselves, the other person, and reality in a very different way than we normally do. We feel altered for a time, but after a while, the structures of the self reassert themselves and the ego returns to its normal condition. This may be one reason why many couples don't stay in love for long. The condition of being "in love" in this heightened way is ultimately intolerable for the ego because it implies both a vulnerability and a lack of control. Because that barrier to feeling our wanting reconstructs itself, things return to what we think of as normal, and that fresh and wonderful feeling starts to dim.

From the limited perspective of the ego, reality is separated from the presence of our natural condition of consciousness, which is a sense of sufficiency, fullness, and presence. For the ego, wanting and desiring always imply an inherent lack, a feeling that something is missing in oneself that perhaps another will satisfy. We have already spent some time looking at love—its richness and depth, and how it is ever flowing and ever present. But some of you mentioned feeling the need to be loved arising as a big, open maw. Falling in love with someone begins as a wanting, a desiring, and a loving: "I feel great when I first fall in love; it feels rich and full and there's no problem; I can just let it flow." But then there's the flip side—you start to feel disconnected and then the need comes up: "I want that feeling back . . . I don't have it . . . I need it . . . Where can I get it? Oh, there it is—I want that!" The sense of not having dominates. You want to grab it to get it back, and if it does come back, you do everything you can to hold on to it. Or you might do the opposite and try to resist those urges, pretending that you don't need anything. Maybe you swing back and forth between the two.

This is similar to our relationship to our inner condition—how we feel about ourselves even when another person isn't in the picture. Our wanting and desire have so many layers over them that the original feeling is nowhere to be found; what remains are our ideas encasing the feeling of love and desire and distorting the experience. This is how we play games and manipulate, control, and restrict ourselves with regard to neediness, love, or desire. The stronger the force of desire, the more our associated feelings and resistances come into play. But the main source of difficulty is not the way we manage our experience consciously; it is the unconsciousness of our conditioned self.

When we allow ourselves to fully experience our wanting, and we trust that the wanting itself has the intelligence to reveal the pure energy of desire that underlies it, we get a taste of what it's like to feel love and desire as a unified force. We experience both the feeling of love and the power that is in it. And we don't even have to fall in love for that to happen. Falling in love is one condition that helps us to experience love and desire as a unified force, one of the main ways of experiencing divine eros. But the capacity to experience divine eros is a potential that lives in all of us, whether or not we are sharing love with another person. This loving desire, which is often first ignited by our human relationships, is a characteristic of all real love relationships, including our relationship to true nature.

When we feel the desire to know our nature, we may not conceptualize that desire in those words. A flame is lit, and we experience the wish to know more, see more, be more, feel more. We want to become more consciously aware of what we internally sense to be our potential. We want to discover the depth and meaning in life and existence. As the presence of something beyond awakens in us, a desire to be close to that something also awakens; a wanting to find out about it arises. It might begin as an interest, but some sort of desire is present even in an intellectual interest. A little intellectual desire can open us up and become a draw toward experiencing what is beyond our conventional perspective.

Regardless of the entry point, you will find that as your inquiry deepens, a sense of emptiness typically emerges at some point. This is an encounter with the limits of the conventional realm of experience. It is a feeling of a lack, of wanting something you don't have, even if you don't know exactly what it is. You start to sense that you are out of touch, and you feel a desire or drive to be in touch with something real, in touch with reality. In order to move through this experience of emptiness into a true fullness of love, we need to better understand how the ego keeps us disconnected from our true nature. So let's go deeper in our exploration of the experience of emptiness and how it can lead us to true eros.

Exploring Deficient Emptiness

As far as the ego is concerned, desire, need, and wanting are all bound up together—maybe with a little love thrown in, because, even on an ego level, we don't desire something we don't like. We don't think, "Oh, I really want that . . . I don't like it." No, we think, "I like it; that is why I want it." So we like, we love, we want, but underneath—and usually not in our awareness—is an emptiness that we defend against. This contributes to the belief that we need to have the object of our desire to fill the emptiness, which can take us into forbidden territory: As we get in touch with the wanting and the desiring, angst often accompanies them, and our longing brings out a need that sometimes can make us feel infantile or deficient because that kind of wanting comes from a very deep place of emptiness.

What is that emptiness? It is a way of experiencing the lack of connection to our true nature. In our natural condition, when we are connected we are open and available to the presence of Being and the pure openness of the void, the two sides of our true nature. The void side of true nature is not lacking in any way. It is the simple, clear purity of openness itself, without which true selfless love is not possible. From the inherent potential in this openness can arise a love that is a giving, loving fullness. However, when the presence of our nature is missing and we feel the disconnection, we feel emptiness. This emptiness is not spacious, open, clear, and bright. No, this is a deficient emptiness, which is more a dull, murky darkness accompanied by the specific sense of lack. "I don't have love; I don't have sufficiency; something is missing . . ." This territory is difficult for us because we sense that if we really feel the desire and need, it will take us into that deficient emptiness—and it can! The two go hand in hand: The need and the emptiness are two sides of the same thing. So we desire something to fill the emptiness, and we become focused on having to get something that will do that.

But if we actually feel the need and desire, and we follow them to the underlying energetic presence, we find that it is much more than we originally felt it to be. Just as it is with love, following our feelings invites the emptiness to open up, and this emptiness then can become the conduit for change because it is the beginning of the appearance of the spaciousness of our true nature.

Desire, on any level you feel it, has a real energy to it, doesn't it? It is not something you are blasé about. No, when you want something, you feel an urgency, an intensity: "I really, really want this, even though I may not let anyone see that." You want it so much that you want to grab it fully, completely. If you really allow those feelings, you feel your whole body full of desire, and you want to eat up that object of your wanting—"It's *mine!*"

Our wanting usually is quite self-centered to begin with, which is one reason why we might resist feeling it. But we need to allow ourselves to be in the condition in which our desire initially arises. It always begins with somebody wanting something. Good! There's a self that wants something! Feel it. Don't push it away. We are not pursuing some spiritual ideal of becoming a selfless being who doesn't want anything. It is the truth we are after. If this is what is there, we must confront it and understand it. We don't yet know that our wanting can be transformed into the pure energy of desire, but if we suppress our feelings at any point along the way, we lose the opportunity to focus on the truth of our experience, to find out more about what it means.

Yes, there is emptiness, and there are feelings of deficiency because of what we believe we don't have. Thus we don't let ourselves feel our desires, because we believe that they will never be met; we keep telling ourselves that it doesn't make sense to want something that we can't have. How many times do you tell yourself that? A desire might spring up in you for something or someone, but you push it down: "I can't get the job, so why go there?" or "He doesn't want me, so I'm not going to feel that I want him." Some people don't even get as far as feeling the desire. Just an inkling of the wanting trips an automatic switch inside, and the feeling doesn't even surface. But we could do something different and simply let the feeling be there whether our desire is met or not. What would that be like?

When you really let yourself want something and you bring your focus back to the experience of the wanting itself, at some point you start to feel that you are *alive* with wanting. You are fully alive with an energetic, bubbling, sparkling, effulgent wanting: "Oh my God, this feels really good. I feel *alive*. I am finally letting myself feel this thing that I haven't let myself feel since the day that person rejected me . . . or the time when this thing didn't happen . . . or the day I was so disappointed when I didn't get that thing I worked so hard for." If you keep allowing that feeling, the focus on the outer drops away and you are able to feel the feeling of pure desire itself. Desire has a bubbling, energetic quality that has a fullness to it, a full, dynamic feeling. It is sparkling, bright, tingly, effervescent.

Getting in touch with that energy is a way to unleash the fullness and sufficiency of the sense of divine eros that is naturally a giving. A transformation begins to happen: Your desire is no longer just about wanting to pull something toward you. You feel passionate, but your focus is no longer on getting your needs met by some outside object. Now you don't just want to get love, you also want to give yourself, to pour yourself out: "I'm giving this all that I have and all that I am!!" Desire becomes a moving out of yourself toward what you love. The love you feel is overflowing, and now it is also full and sweet. All of the possibilities and potentials of being in touch with your own energy allow the love to flower. *The love fills out the desire with itself.*

I'll tell you about the first time I woke up to this myself. I was about thirty years old, and the object of my desire was a man I thought I couldn't ever become involved with. It was very clear that it wasn't going to happen. One night, I sat alone in my house, weepy and sad, thinking, "I'm going to be in my little house by myself for the rest of my life." I began to feel the sinking gravity of spiraling down into the depressing darkness of aloneness. I was grumpy and cranky, desiring and longing. And I was arguing with myself—with the internal voices of what we sometimes refer to in the work as the superego, the inner critic, or the judge. The judge was giving me all the reasons why I should stop thinking about this man and get on with my pathetic life (which was actually not at all pathetic).

Finally I said to myself, "Okay, I don't give a damn about any of that—I want him! I want him and that's the way it is. I feel what I feel, and I'm going to keep feeling it. And nobody can get in my way. This is what is happening." I almost shut down again because I was mortified at the thought that someone might see me this way. But then, as though someone were there listening that I needed to convince, I said, "He is not here, so I can feel anything I want." I used the Gestalt Therapy technique of imagining him sitting on a pillow opposite me, and I said out loud, "I want you and I love you. So come and get me—I dare you!" and then, "I want you and I'm going to get you."

Soon I started to feel a tingling bubble up, an effervescence, a thrilling feeling of love: "I love you so much that I'm going to eat you up and smother you with my love; I'm going to ooze the sweetness of it and melt you . . ." And I let it rip. I let it all happen right there. I felt all of it, as much as I wanted to. And that felt completely natural and right. It was a deeply emotional experience . . . at first, a rippling feeling, and then fireworks—exploding, brilliant fireworks—and shivering. And then I started to feel this thrill, an effulgent, thick sweetness. Along with that came a sparkling dynamism—"I feel so pure . . . I feel vibrant, I feel alive, I feel full. I have found what I wanted." I was in tears. Something from inside had come forward, and I realized that this was the feeling I had wanted all along by wanting to have him. I had met my lover. The Beloved had come to me in the way it willed, not in the way I thought I wanted. I was touched in a very deep way. I felt present. I felt full, alive, and thrilled by my very existence. This was one of the happiest, most meaningful moments of my life. It opened me to the heart that is the celebration of Living Being.

Because I followed my experience inward rather than in the usual outward direction, desire led me to communion with my nature in an explosive, exciting, thrilling, beautiful way. It all started with a feeling of need, of needing to have something, of needing to take in the object of desire to fulfill me. At first, I felt empty, lacking, needy, and deficient. But at some point, the energy itself became my focus of interest. I wanted to know my experience as fully as possible regardless of the outcome. Everything turned around when I felt my heart splayed wide open with pain and longing and was able to allow those feelings, to feel them fully. Then I saw that I had been waiting for this man to be there to respond to my need so that I could feel what I was feeling now, and that this could limit me indefinitely. I found myself saying, "I'm sick of letting these feelings sit there and I'm sick of not having them embraced. I'm going to embrace them

myself. I'm going to sit here and feel all of this for as long as it takes."
I allowed my attention to embrace the experience of desire, rather
than expecting the object of my desire to fulfill me. I welcomed the
truth of my experience to come and overtake me fully. What I discovered was not only my love—I discovered the truth.

Exploding into the Source

I had thought the object of my desire was a man or a person, but
what the experience revealed was that my wanting was arising as a
natural movement toward its source—the source of all consciousness, which includes me. This source—the ocean of dynamic, fluid
energy that is the deeper nature of all of us—was presencing into
the moment as the one who is me. We don't ever pop out of our
true nature and become something else; we remain part of the
source because we are inseparable from it, even though we each
experience it through our individual consciousness. Experiencing
this opened me to a whole new realm of possibilities. And it showed
me that desire, at its root, is the energy of our deeper nature, an
explosive energy that is dynamic and rich and bubbling forward.
When my attention embraced the experience of desire rather than
the object of my desire, I was able to know the truth of that nature
as myself.

This energy of desire is also the force behind manifestation. We
are here because this force is birthing us into existence right now,
exploding and arising at this moment. At each point in our experience, we are exploding into now, nakedly, purely. And this now *is*
the presence of this dynamic force that at this very moment is birthing us into existence. So one of the ways we experience the force of
manifestation through individual consciousness is as desire. Any-
time we feel a desire, it can open up the potential for the qualities of
our nature to arise. Desire is the force that calls us toward something we don't know, that leads us to what is beyond that which
we're wanting.

One of the main ways the vibrating, scintillating, throbbing quality of our Being can express itself is as desire. When we want something, our desire is pushing itself up for recognition as the dynamism of our being; what fuels the wanting for that person or object or situation is always rooted in the energy of Being itself. But we tend to get caught up in the content of the desire rather than staying in touch with the fact that desire itself is starting to well up. Desire is the expression of the true energy of Being. When felt fully, it reveals itself and reconnects consciousness with its origins.

When the energy of true desire combines with the fluid sweetness of love, we feel the presence of love and the generosity of heart together with the wanting and the desire—all as one unified presence. We experience an effulgently sparkling energetic presence. The desiring has a feeling of fullness in it. It is no longer a desire out of need; it is a robust fullness, a sweetness, an expression of love. It originates from connectedness, from presence, from being the now. Desiring is now coupled with generosity, and it is both giving and receptive of the gifting. A dance of a giving way of loving, and a bubbling delight of desire, now becomes possible. Desire runs wild with the interest and joy of discovery in the moment. Whether in relation to another person or not, the desire can arise and magnetically draw us near the source. We find ourselves wanting to know, discover, explore, find out about life, the world, and the inner world: What is this dance going to be like? What is this day going to bring? What will I find? What am I? How will I know you differently today? How will I know myself? What will it mean? How can we interact?

This energy is fresh, clean, pure, new, vibrant, and robust. When we want to fill a need it is a mere echo of this energy, just the ringing of emptiness when the energy is not felt. What is present in need that is also in this pure desire? The need has an energy that we can connect to if we give ourselves permission to feel our desires fully and completely. It is important to understand that the energy inherent in desire shows itself through our experience, which is influenced by our past, so generally it emerges with our needs as well as our ideas about who we are and who the other is. But if we allow ourselves to feel the desires that arise out of deficiency or need, we can follow that thread back to its source, and the energy will keep exploding those old ideas until what remains is only pure energy.

And pure energy does not judge itself. It just is. It is a pure expression of something that is innately yours. It is your life force. It is your life energy, and it brings life, a dynamic effulgence, to your love so that the love and the energy become one. The dancing together is so intimate and complete that there is no difference between the love and the energy.

So we need to suspend our ideas about what can come forward. We need to not judge our needs, because it is necessary to explore everything in our experience. Even though it can be painful, it is important to allow the neediness that is mixed with desire to come into consciousness. That's because the desire, in and of itself, is a way back—back to our energetic heart, back to that erotic, alive, and full energy waiting to burst out with the joy and exuberance of life and love and desire as one. We are getting close here to what we mean by divine eros.

As we have seen, we tend to clamp our feelings down with all kinds of notions about what might happen. This kills the opportunity to fully experience life, love, and the great exhilaration of creating each moment, which is the potential of what we are. This is why it is important to keep sensing your belly without either acting out your feelings or suppressing them. Repressing desire simply makes our consciousness thick, and we remain unaware of this potential. So don't repress the energy—but you don't want to let it express itself impulsively either. You want to be able to just be with it. Ride the wave and feel your feet on the ground . . .

Judgments or fear may be coming up for you as you absorb what is being said here. That's fine. Allow whatever you are experiencing. You want to unveil the truth of what is. So shine the light of awareness on the experience that is present now. By investigating your experience, you can begin to remove some of the thick layers that encase your fresh, vibrant, and alive love. Through understanding the unconscious dynamics involved, you can clarify the obscured and distorted beliefs and patterns underlying them, and divest yourself of the heaviness that restricts your openness to this ecstatic, vibrant, awake, scintillating clarity, which is inseparable from loving sweetness.

EXPLORATION SESSION

In this exercise, you are invited to explore your own experience of desire, so that you can begin to understand the limits you have placed on your experience. When you identify what these limits are, you can open them up to reveal new ways of knowing in a fresh experiential way.

Spend ten or fifteen minutes contemplating each of the following questions, using the directions below as a guide. Each question has a logic that leads to the next, so it is important to ask and respond to them in order.

1. What limits your experience of desire?
2. What is something that you desire?
3. What do you like about desiring?

There are many admonitions against allowing the feeling of desire, so take some time to contemplate how these limits appear in your experience. How do you feel in your body when you consider desire? What do you feel in your chest, belly, even your head? Allowing yourself to fully feel the desire for something can open up your experience of the whole range of feelings that are connected with that desire.

As we have discussed, the desire will initially arise conflated with the object. You want to invite that. The practice is to stay in touch with the visceral, sensate experience of desire as you allow your mind to have its associated ideas about what you desire. You want to deepen your understanding and your ability to discern the difference between the particular desire itself and the energy of desire.

If you are doing this exploration alone, writing or even verbally recording your exploration can be useful. If you are doing it with a partner, alternate asking each other the questions in sequence: Partner A asks partner B the first question and when it is answered, asks it again repeatedly for fifteen minutes. Then partner B asks partner A the same question for fifteen minutes. Do the same for the second and third questions. If you are in a group of three or more, one person can read the question aloud, and each person in the circle will respond in turn, giving one answer. Continue going around the circle for fifteen minutes answering the first question, then do the same for the other two. This method can stimulate an energetic vortex in the group so that each answer builds on the energy of the one before it.

QUESTIONS AND COMMENTS

Student: You told us that desiring is a natural condition, but is it not a way of saying, "I am not happy at this moment, and the future must be better"?

Karen: It can be. Desire shows up whenever we want anything. We have desires for all kind of things: We desire food when we are hungry; we want love when we feel loveless. Some desires are based on a lack. Sometimes that lack is a physical need, such as for food or rest or something else necessary for our survival. Other times, it is an emotional feeling of lack—we are not happy with a certain condition or situation, so we desire something else and hope that the future will bring us what we want. However, if you actually feel the energy of desire, then whether or not there is a lack, the desire can lead you to the underlying energy itself, which isn't based in lack. That is what I was trying to say—desire is part of the natural flow of the energy of life.

We can have a desire that is dissociated from our ground of presence, which is when we feel a lack and are unhappy about it, so we desire something to fix it, change it, or fill it. But if we allow the energy of that desire and follow it to its source, we can feel that this energy actually arises from something that is sufficient, that is truly a fullness. In recognizing the energetic source of desire, we feel it mixed with love. We feel that we love something because we desire it, and we desire it because we love it. Love and desire dance together. Then desire is no longer oriented toward the future; it is expressing a reality now.

But what did you find out for yourself in asking the questions?

Student: I found out that I think I don't have desires.

Karen: Are you happy about that?

Student: Yeah, I'm happy.

Karen: So when you say you don't have desires, what do you feel you are wanting by being here?

Student: Good question. You can call it a desire, maybe, to enjoy the moment more, and maybe I'm here to learn how I can enjoy the moment more.

Karen: Maybe you will . . .

Student: I just want to say that the experience of desire was the start of everything for me. Without desire there wouldn't be anything. I didn't know that before. I don't remember if you told us this, but at least I discovered it, and that was really, really great.

Karen: That is better than anything I tell you—you discovered it for yourself. So what do you feel? What do you mean when you say that it is the beginning?

Student: It means that it is something in my belly . . . it's orange and it's very hot.

Karen: So it feels hot for you?

Student: Yes, and it's safe in a way. I think I thought that desire was in a way unsafe, not only because I like to desire but because there were some desires that were unsafe . . . and right now I don't think so, I don't feel so. And it's nice.

Karen: It feels pleasurable, doesn't it?

Student: Yes. And I'm excited to see what is going to happen.

Karen: It brings a new feeling, an excitement.

Student: Yes, that's the most I have felt it.

Karen: We stop feeling the energy of desire as desire per se. The energy of desire has a thrilling, exciting feeling to it, but it can also feel very pleasurable, slow, and burbling. It isn't necessarily loud and bursting; it can be very quiet and dynamic.

Student: And sweet.

Karen: So you feel sweet as well. The feeling of eros has the energy of desire with sweetness, where there is a blissful kind of pleasure in the love. We can feel a full wanting, which is not the kind of desire we are used to thinking of—the kind that feels like a lack. So you are feeling some fullness?

Student: Yes, yes.

Student: I was really very, very surprised, because when you were talking about this earlier, I thought, "Well, maybe she is right and maybe she isn't," but then I was talking with my partner and it was exactly the same as what you said. It was so fresh and energetic. I could describe now so many things about it . . . but I felt this freedom, joy, and pleasure. It was amazing, and I am very happy that I could feel desire as energy. Thank you very much for that.

Karen: Thank yourself; it is your discovery. It is good that you were open but didn't believe me, and you found out for yourself.

Student: I would like to share something, because when I started to make a distinction between desires coming from egoistic sources and desires coming from the soul, I found out all of a sudden that recognizing desires from my soul is a kind of self-recognition. I can recognize myself in feeling these desires. I was finding myself through these desires, and it felt great. It was wonderful—just letting them come up and saying, "Jesus! This is *me*!" I just wanted to share that with you.

Karen: What are you feeling right now?

Student: Happy.

Karen: Feeling our desires can liberate the heart, because we usually restrain it by not letting ourselves feel the things we want and desire. So feeling those things can bring a lot of joy and freedom.

Student: And stillness. Just the recognition . . .

Karen: I heard a lot of giggling going on, too.

Student: I discovered that I connected being desirous with being dependent. Realizing this somehow freed my desire, and I feel very relieved and actually quite excited about it.

Karen: That is a good insight. Dependency is one of the biggest needy feelings we have, and when we begin to liberate the energy of desire, dependency is one of the feelings that can arise. We feel that we have to have the other; we feel dependent on the other; and this can bring out all kinds of wanting and desirousness, the same feelings we had early in life when we *were* very dependent. We could now recognize that dependency is just a feeling like any other . . . but instead, we get afraid of the feeling. So, now that you feel it, what happens for you?

Student: I feel excited, and when I see those colors over there, I feel that they could somehow explode like a volcano. It is very freeing.

Karen: Dependency never looked so good! For some reason, when we start feeling our dependency, we think that we are going to latch on to somebody and not let go, that we'll become totally dependent or else so needy that we will scare people away. But if we actually allow the feeling without acting on it, we can move through it and feel the desire just as you are expressing it. It can be very liberating to admit to ourselves that we have those desires.

As we have already discussed, in many spiritual traditions, desire is considered negative because it is seen as an ego desire, which is a desire based on our animalistic impulses, our need to survive. Generally, it is recommended that you not feel desires, that you push them aside or just witness them, and continue staying focused on the practice rather than attend to the content. This is suggested so that you don't get distracted by feelings, thoughts, and memories that can bring up a lot of inner conflict. As you see, there is a great deal of difficulty in just allowing the feeling itself. But the truth is that once we allow the feeling, we can understand it and allow it to fulfill its destiny. We have to learn how to do this in a way that optimizes our spiritual realization.

Even so, we need to understand that not all desire is the same. For most individuals, desire and grasping onto the object of desire are the same thing. Desire that is related to attachment is suffering, and it keeps us dissociated from our nature; this type of desire has mostly to do with the self and its object of desire, not with the desiring itself. But as we have seen, desire can function as an avenue to our nature—if we can use the desiring energy that is usually directed outward, thereby creating attachment, to go inward. It takes a determination and a love for the truth to stay with that energy and follow it back to its origin, thereby liberating the energy of desire to serve freedom instead of keeping us bound in suffering.

And that is what we are trying to do here—harness that energy, feel it fully. Even the smallest desire has a trickle of that energy, so experiencing that wanting and following it inward, feeling the energy of it, can release our mind from the content of the desire. Just staying with the energy will naturally open up into a deeper level of our existence, and this is the naturalness of the process.

So if we want to be ourselves completely—to know our nature at its depth and be fully in the world—this requires being alive and being in touch with that energy. And that brings the erotic into love. In other words, to be able to experience divine eros, we need the purity of love, the ground of lovingness and goodness, the experience of the presence of love, plus this scintillating, erupting, explosive quality that has an energy to it. Such energetic dynamic love can be very, very fine—like very gentle bubbles or a gentle vibration—or it can be explosive. This love has an erotic quality to it, and we can feel it draw us toward the divine, toward the truth, toward our inner nature. We can have the experience of desiring to penetrate the mystery, to know the spirit.

A deep understanding of reality can follow from such a realization of desire. We can see that dualism arises when we are separated from our nature, for it is then that we experience the desire to fill ourselves. We believe there is something external that we need to have, and we deeply believe that we don't have that something. However, with the energy of desire, when we feel it as the blissful wanting of another—but with a sense of sufficiency, not from lack—we don't feel the same kind of otherness we do when we have a dualistic perspective. We feel that the other is arising from the same ground as we are. There is a sharing of a blissful communion, and that communion is a recognition that both of you are one reality.

We can also feel a loving desire toward our essential nature as the Beloved. Then we are in a dance with that nature, an ebb and a flow with it, and we are not separate—nor are we one. There is enough differentiation for us to feel the excitement of moving toward the Beloved again. We feel that we are, in a sense, ourselves in union. It is nice to appear as two, but it doesn't mean that there are two. So the appearance of two is what allows the love to have that vigorous feeling of wanting another and the enjoyment of wanting. There is a fullness to this desire, and you know that within each other, you are the same. A dualistic or a monistic view alone keeps us from the recognition that our nature is a continuous unity within which we can view and appreciate one another as a manifestation of reality, recognizing that the Beloved is what you are in union with.

MUSIC MEDITATION

Suggested Selection:

"Niobe's Theme" from the album *Rome: Music from the HBO Series* (soundtrack CD by Jeff Beal)

Let's end with a music meditation. Settle in, relax, and feel your belly. Just let yourself be wherever you are in relation to desire, however you are experiencing it. Even a mental wish to know something is an expression of a desire. Let whatever is there be there as you sense your belly. You may be feeling desire for your nature, a particular thing or person, for God, for essence. You may be wanting to know the truth, to know spirit, to know what is beyond you. You may feel the presence of the desire itself at this moment. Whatever it is, just let yourself feel it. And let yourself feel free to move with the music; let yourself be moved by wherever you are.

5

Personal Relationships

HAMEED

PERHAPS IT IS OBVIOUS that humanity is still at the beginning of actualizing its potential. We can see that we are not that far into the process of maturation. As part of our human potential, we can be completely transparent, like air; a feeling or inner experience can arise in a completely free way, totally unimpeded, unrestricted, undistorted. The spontaneity, transparency, and fullness of our experience can be present whatever experience we have—whatever emotion, whatever thought, whatever perception—for when we are in a completely natural condition, experiences arise as manifestations of our radiance, of our true light. However, we often have difficulty experiencing much of what arises in our experience as clearly as we might; we have difficulty seeing things for what they are—even things we feel very deeply about. This has had profound consequences for human beings throughout our history, and has caused much suffering and pain.

We might be able to recognize that the history of humanity is a sorrowful and painful one, but recognizing this doesn't mean that we're free to feel everything about it. Our hearts are not completely free to feel everything that naturally will arise within us. For example, many of us just saw how it's not always easy to experience desire. As we discussed, many spiritual teachings advocate becoming free from desire—but how are we going to be free from something that we haven't yet allowed ourselves to experience? The same is true with suffering and emotional pain: How can we be free from our pain if we don't allow ourselves to experience it? How are we going to be free from our anger if we don't allow ourselves to feel it? If we don't allow ourselves to experience a feeling, we are saying no to that part of our experience; and if we say no, we are not free; we are not transparent, and we don't experience the luminosity, the light of our spiritual nature.

The Challenge of Relating

Much of our difficulty, much of our human struggle, has to do with other human beings—that is, how we feel in relation to other people. In engaging a spiritual path, we need to explore all of our experience, everything in our lives, but it is particularly important to inquire into a central aspect of life that we deal with every day, one that brings us difficulty and promise but also a unique possibility. While it is true that a lot of our pain and suffering is connected to occurrences such as accidents and physical illness, the fact that we relate to each other, talk to each other, interact, and have relationships of various kinds is behind much of the pain and suffering of humanity.

Human beings do more harm to one another than to anything else in their world. And our lack of inner transparency is mainly connected to the difficulties we have with other individuals. The difficulties we have experienced in our personal history—especially in our upbringing, our early childhood—mostly have to do with other people. You rarely see somebody having a great deal of difficulty in his life because of dissatisfaction with the inanimate objects of his past, such as a toothbrush or pillow, for example. Teddy bears, dolls, might bring up some painful memories and feelings, but this is not the primary source of our suffering. Those kinds of issues don't arise in inner work unless interactions with people impacted and influenced the child's relationship to these things. What comes up more often are feelings about family life—our relations with father and mother, sisters and brothers, uncles and aunts—and with society and the people in it.

Because relationships are so important for us humans, we need to not only consider them in terms of what happens when we relate to the people in our lives, but also to understand relationship as a whole, as a context that creates our mind, creates our sense of self, shapes how we see the world. Relationships can constrict and limit the way we see ourselves and the world or else they can become windows through which we can see more clearly who we are, what the world is, what the possibilities of life are.

On the path of spiritual realization, as we come to know ourselves at deeper levels—as we recognize our presence, our spirit, our inner light, our love—the next step is to know how to bring all of this into the world, how to live it. And the primary way of doing that is in relation to other people. It may be difficult to ride your bicycle in the enlightened condition, but you will notice that this is much easier than interacting with your husband or wife. Things are more complex when it comes to other human beings. Your bicycle doesn't change—it is always the same. Or once in a while something happens and you fix it—but it is quite predictable. Another human being is a whole universe, a complex and rich set of possibilities. We usually don't fully recognize that fact; we don't let ourselves see or appreciate it. However, when you explore and experience yourself more thoroughly, you see how much there is to your consciousness—and it is the same with everybody else. The riches innate to our soul, which relationships can limit or invite, are the same for all souls, all human beings.

Our spiritual realization is more complete when we bring our realization, our presence, our compassion, our clarity and understanding into interaction with others. This includes how we talk with one another, how we respond, how we touch, how we allow ourselves to be touched, what we do and don't do and how and when we do it, so that our life with other people can express the inner freedom we have attained. True inner freedom is not abstract. Freedom means the freedom to express the qualities of our nature, the freedom to express our love, our joy, our kindness, our strength, our intelligence, our sensitivity. Freedom does not mean just that we feel light, happy, and free. That is wonderful, but it is only the beginning of inner freedom, of enlightenment, of realization.

On the path of the Diamond Approach, realization is complete and mature when we experience the freedom of the realized condition in our functioning and relating. This is the actualized side of realization: I do not lose myself when interacting with others—that is, I do not lose what I truly am, the truth I discovered in my awakening—but rather I continue to be myself with the person I am interacting with, whether I am living with them, talking with them, working with them, playing with them, or traveling with them. I am myself, I am authentic, I am real, and I am also responsive and interactive in a way that expresses what I truly am. I recognize that there is something unique about me, just as I recognize there is something unique about each one of you.

True nature is the same in all of us, but the way it comes through, the way we integrate it, what we learn from it, and what we become because of it is different for each one of us. Our true nature has so many qualities, so many capacities, so many skills, and so many possibilities, that each person turns out to be a unique manifestation of that ground of reality, that underlying ocean of Being. It is an ocean that has no shores, no beaches. It doesn't have an end. But it has many waves, and every one of them is a being—and each being is different from every other.

What do we need in order to learn about love and eros—divine eros—and about the role of love and wanting and desire? How can we embrace the excitement of life with all its pleasure and enjoyment? We need to experience and express all of these things, and this happens mostly in relationship with other people. You can definitely have an enjoyable experience with your cat or your dog. Many people have wonderful experiences with nature and with animals. But with human beings, relating is more difficult, though the potential is far greater.

SPIRITUAL NATURE IN RELATIONSHIP

The spiritual dimension can manifest in our lives to enrich our relating and make it more real, and the reverse is also true. If we approach our relationships with openness and sincerity, with the true sense of who we are—if we are authentic and respect the authenticity of the other; if we listen to and are interested in one another just as we are interested in the truth—then any relationship can contribute to our spiritual experience. It can become a support for our spiritual journey, a crucible for inner work. Relationship can become a natural practice that deepens both our sense of who we are and our experience of reality. An understanding of divine eros brings those two aspects together in such a way that spiritual realization can contribute to relationship and relationship can contribute to spiritual realization.

However, for that to happen, our relationships will need to become transparent to our spiritual qualities. By this we mean that it is not sufficient that the soul or consciousness is transparent to its spiritual qualities, which means these qualities can come through our consciousness and be expressed without obstruction. The relationship as a whole—which is both the contact between me and you and the energetic field created by our interaction—will need to manifest those qualities. So there needs to be not only enjoyment between the two people but also sincerity and authenticity—a real individual interacting with another real individual.

What is a real individual? A person who is aware of who he or she is, and who is being that authentic presence in interaction with another person, while respecting that the other is also authentic presence. That is what I call a sense of being personal—what is personally me interacting with what is personally you. It is the uniqueness of my reality interacting with the uniqueness of your reality.

Our spirit, in its transcendent nature, in its unity, is impersonal, which means that it is universal, limitless; but the way it expresses itself in relationship is very personal. It's the very essence of personalness. This personalness has a sense of true, direct contact, a feeling of immediate in-touchness with the other. When I am interacting with another person, I feel that my soul is touching her soul. It sometimes feels to me much more immediate than my hand touching that person; it feels more full, more complete.

A relationship between two people can be more or less real. Not only can we both be personally real, our relationship can be real. For that to happen, however, a relationship will need to express the qualities of true nature. You may notice in all of our explorations the implicit principle that our spiritual essence has a sense of perfection, goodness, and purity that is beyond who we are as individuals and is the source of all the beautiful, positive qualities that we think are most human—in the sense of being most expressive of the human heart. It is the generous love, the selfless compassion, the courage, the clear discernment of a situation, the exercise of intelligence, that all lead to the discovery and arising of new knowledge, new insight. These are human qualities, but more fundamentally they are our spiritual qualities.

If we are to learn about divine eros, we need to see that it arises mostly between two in interaction. It can arise between the soul and her true nature, as love that has a pleasurable, enjoyable, erotic quality—in the sense that it is an energy with desire and pleasure and sensuousness in it. But when divine eros arises between two people, we understand how human relationship is a form in which those qualities can arise most fully and completely.

In general, humanity is not well developed in its capacity for personal relating. We have a lot of trouble with violence, aggression, misunderstanding, disappointment, pain, wounding, and so on—all of it because we are not good at relationships. It is very easy to misunderstand somebody and get angry and become aggressive, or feel hurt, withdraw, and run away. But to remain in a relationship, to be real and interact in a way that not only avoids contraction or pain but that opens things up, that generates more richness, creates more openness and more freedom, is something that human beings are just beginning to learn. Throughout history, some people have been very good at that, but as a race, we are still immature. Humanity is just beginning to wake up to the importance of relationship and its amazing potential. This potential is immense, both for creating peace in the world and for personal actualization of human completeness.

How are you going to actualize your compassion if it is not with other people? How are you going to actualize your love if not with other people? How are you going to realize, actualize, and embody your courage if it is not with other people? These days, it is rare that you would need courage for encountering a bear on the road; we usually need the courage to face a person, not a bear or a lion or a tiger.

If we want to experience and express—either in general or with another person—divine eros, if we want that wonderful, pleasurable, turned-on quality in our lives, it is important for us to recognize, understand, and allow ourselves to open to experiencing some qualities that are specific to human relationships.

DISCOVERING PERSONAL CONTACT

First, we need to learn what it means to be truly personal. We need to value our contact with another person. Contact is not just an exchange of information. Two computers can exchange information. They don't care about contact—contact will actually interfere with their operation. For human beings, sharing information is useful, often important, but the quality of contact is what really matters; that's what makes us human and will make our relationships either develop into something richer, bigger, deeper, or else limit and diminish them.

True contact requires a sense that there is connection, a unity between us, or at least that we have an interest or desire to experience our closeness, our connectedness, our interrelatedness. In connecting with another human being, we can experience a great deal of depth, a great deal of texture in our experience, in our consciousness, with many varieties, flavors, and shades of color and light. The erotic sphere is one particular arena that requires all of these. We cannot have divine eros in our relationship if our relationship is superficial, if the contact is not comfortable, not real. There needs to be a sense of a connection, a bond: "Yeah, I feel very close to you, and I am interested in knowing you and knowing what is really going on with you. Not because I want to fix something, or because I want to be a good person or not feel guilty, but because I really want to know you. For when I know you, I feel my contact with you, and I can feel how we are one in our true humanity."

The sense of connectedness and contact and the sense of personalness are what characterize a true relationship. These qualities of personalness, contact, and connection are necessary for divine eros to emerge in the interactive field. Divine eros is deep and subtle and requires a great deal of authenticity in the contact between two people; otherwise, it says, "Not interested! This is not a hospitable environment . . . this consciousness is too crude for me . . ."

In addition, to have a relationship of true personalness, true contact—whether you have eye contact, physical contact, or just consciousness contact—both the quality of presence and the communication need to also have an openness in which neither person is trying to defend himself or herself, or selfishly trying to gain an advantage. Instead, each person is committed to being authentic and allowing both parties to find out what is possible for the relationship.

For this to happen, we need to approach relationship in the same way that we approach our own personal experience—from a perspective of openness and curiosity, so that we can find out what our relationship is. We can say to ourselves, "What is this relationship? Who are we? What is happening right now between us? I am curious to know. I want to know myself and I want to know you. And I want to know myself *with* you. I want to know how you feel with me and how the two of us, as we come to know each other, feel together, because these are important truths and I value knowing them." This attitude requires an openness that has no defensiveness, does not try to protect itself. It needs the kind of trust that takes time and honest communication—trust that comes from a sincere interest that arises out of the connection because we care about the quality of the contact.

This openness and caring is bound to bring up in us a kind of vulnerability and tenderness that most human beings feel ill at ease with. But we cannot be transparent to the divine in its erotic dimension if we don't allow ourselves to be vulnerable. "Vulnerable" means "not defended"; when we are not protecting ourselves, we are free to feel our delicacy. We are free to feel the exquisiteness and softness of our consciousness. If our consciousness is thick, opaque, and dense, then it is self-protective. It is not vulnerable, it is not transparent; subtle qualities and forms in our experience don't freely arise. And most important, we cannot completely receive the other person. We can't feel them, we can't recognize them, and we can't see their uniqueness. We can't see who they are.

When we become truly spiritual, our caring for God becomes our caring for one another, because we see God in each other. We can't say that we care for God and then assume that a person doesn't have God inside them. The person might not know it, might be very blocked—might even be mad and hateful—but deep inside there is only one reality. This person has true nature regardless of how he or she is acting. If we all knew that, if all of humanity knew that, everyone would stop killing each other. We would understand that it would be like killing somebody we deeply love; it would be like killing oneself.

We want to learn how to be with each other in a way that will deepen and expand the relationship, give it the freedom, the opportunity, to develop its potential. We are implying here that just as our soul can develop, our relationships can develop. A relationship between two people is a kind of soul, a type of field of consciousness; it can either be opaque to its true nature or else it can be transparent to it, allowing the luminosity of true nature to manifest within and through it. Such transparency requires both people to be sincere in their interaction, caring about what happens in and to the field. They recognize that "In the same way that I care about my soul and how it is going to manifest, I care about the soul of my interaction with you. I have the opportunity here to discover and experience your truth, and mine, and to learn how we can both develop further through our relationship. The more I come to know you, the more I come to know myself."

When we are by ourselves, we experience our authenticity differently than when we are with another. And our experience of being with someone varies depending on whom we are with. We can be authentic and real in any situation, but what arises in us will differ depending on whether we are alone or interacting—and each interaction is unique. So each relationship, each interaction, is an opportunity for life to manifest its possibilities. It is an opportunity for the arising of divine eros. A mature relationship provides a place where we can express the divine in many different ways, such as friendly and kind, or pleasurable and playful; intimate and peaceful, or erotic and exciting—depending on the context and nature of the relationship.

For a relationship to be real, for it to develop and mature—which means that it becomes a place where we can discover ourselves and learn about the divine—many things are necessary and important. Part of our exploration here involves engaging in exercises to learn how to approach our relationships in a way that enhances our spirituality and also brings our spirituality into the relationships.

EXPLORATION SESSION

We have been learning how to inquire, how to explore our personal experience, and now we can extend that into an inquiry between two people, into their interactive field, into the quality of interaction. The interaction involves communication and much more; it involves contact, openness, interest, mutuality, and reciprocity. It can be in words or subtle, nonverbal cues, or both. Communication and contact can also be of consciousness, of direct presence.

For this exercise, choose a partner with whom you will interact. You will be inquiring into your relationship: how you feel with the other, how the other feels to you or about you, what the quality of the contact is, what the quality of the relationship is as you interact. This will be similar to inquiring into your own personal experience, but here you are inquiring into what is happening between two people. We suggest that you spend twenty minutes in this exploration.

Your interaction, your expression, will of course be appropriate to the situation. By this I mean, for example, that you talk differently to your wife than to your daughter. You talk to your daughter differently than to your friend. Things happen between you and your husband or wife that can't happen between you and your friend. This is one meaning of "appropriate." But regardless of the type of relationship, there can be freedom, there can be genuineness in the interaction.

One of you could start by saying, for example, "I was really touched by that card you sent me. It was very nice of you to think about my mother being in the hospital; it was a difficult time for me."

The other person might respond: "I know . . . I remember . . . I'm glad I did that. I didn't want to do what you did to me the last time my mother was sick."

And your dialogue can go on from there:

"What do you mean?"

"What I mean is that you were insensitive at that time, and it really hurt."

"Oh really—I hurt you?"

"Well, of course; I was really hurt because I thought you were a good friend."

Or it might be something like:

"I don't know you very well, but as I am sitting with you, I feel really comfortable, as though I've known you for a long time."

And the other person says, "Really? I feel I don't know you at all, and for me that is quite delightful."

"What do you mean, 'It is quite delightful'?"

"Well, whatever you say is going to be new to me."

"Give me an example."

"Just your voice makes me feel sort of fresh."

"You like my voice?"

"There is something about when we interact, when I'm talking with you . . . it feels like some kind of harmony happens. And I feel I can talk to you about anything."

"Anything, huh? I don't know if I like that. I am starting to get a little scared about this—what do you mean 'anything'? Do you have something in mind?"

"Well, now that you mention it . . ."

We want to include all kinds of real-life situations. You and your partner for this exercise might be very close to each other or you might know one another only a little bit. Regardless of the type of relationship you currently have, the fact that you are sitting together and talking means that a particular relationship is happening right then. Perhaps your connection with each other has a long history, which can enter into the situation right now. One of you says, "I can't be authentically myself with you because of our last twenty years of history together. I can't get over all that history. I wish Hameed and Karen would take that away."

And the other says, "You know, it was twenty-*one* years!" Some people are very sensitive about those things! "You forgot when we got married. You think it was twenty years ago, but it was twenty-one—and our anniversary, if you don't know, is in a week!"

Whatever our situation, we are open as we talk: There is openness, there is genuineness, there is contact, there is truthfulness; and it is all in a field, a pool of consciousness, that can open up or close down. Whichever happens, it is fine—you just want to explore what's there.

"It seems that we are all tense and don't want to talk to each other. I wonder what happened?"

And the other person says, "I don't really know. I feel the same way. I feel like I want to go away. I want to talk to this other person over there."

"Why? What happened for you?"

Maybe both of you were really shy and, after ten minutes of exploration, you realize that you like each other but you don't want to know that, much less let the other person know, because it means you will be vulnerable. "If I show that I really like you—who knows? Maybe you won't like me." So people get a little protective. All kinds of surprises can happen.

We call this "dialectic inquiry"—there is a dialectic, an interaction of two forces merging together and becoming one vortex, one force. Two souls connect, becoming one. Inquiring into this combined consciousness develops the relationship, and the relationship can become a means of developing the individuals who are in it.

After the period of dialectic inquiry, you can take ten minutes to discuss what qualities arose: Was it contact that developed, was it love, was it kindness, was it openness? You also want to see what stopped these qualities from coming up—what limited them? Sometimes it can be fear, sometimes guilt, sometimes protectiveness. Reflecting together on the dialectic and discussing it will help you arrive at some understanding to see which qualities of true relationship developed during your interaction with your partner.

Questions and Comments

Student: I would like to share an experience I had in the dialectic with someone that I already know for many years. At the end, I noticed suddenly that he is a German guy and I am a Dutch guy, and I realized that he is here on this day in Amsterdam, living around the corner in the Herenstraat. I am feeling both the sense of the history—his history with his family, which I don't know, and the history of my family, which he doesn't know—and the very now-ness of this moment. It felt very *now,* and I felt both the history and a sense of reconciliation in that moment.

Hameed: You are in the now and you are aware of the history. How was the history influencing the experience in the now?

Student: It gave a very special depth to the now, a presence.

Hameed: The history was functioning in such a way that it brought you more deeply into the now instead of obstructing the now. That can happen, yes. Part of our uniqueness comes from our history. Each of us has a unique history, and we are different individuals as a result; we are what we are partly because of our history. Although our nature is beyond our history, our history contributes to the development of our character, how we are with other people.

It seems like there were many conversations going on in your dialectic.

———————————

Student: I noticed that for me it was important to also invite the pain of other people I have excluded in my life. It is very important to make space for this in the meeting with the other. That is what I wanted to tell you.

Hameed: I don't know if I am understanding you. Is it the first time you met the person you did the exercise with?

Student: I didn't know that person before. And I had the sense to make a place for all the persons in my life I have excluded, to invite the pain of that in this meeting also.

Hameed: Interesting. It is interesting how that situation can create an opportunity like that.

Student: It was very touching.

Hameed: I can feel that. Many of us here are touched by our interactions, whether it is with people we know very well or people we don't know very well. Being touched in this way is what I meant by the quality of contact, the quality of interaction.

———————————

6

The Relational Field

KAREN

EROS IS RELEVANT for any human being who is interested in living a full human life, since it is the inherent energy of the zest and sparkle of our life force. Knowing the fundamental nature of our life force is of great importance for the serious spiritual student. And to lead a life of spiritual maturity and full participation in the world, both the knowledge and the embodiment of the nature *and* energy of life are needed. We have already seen that it is not necessary to choose between the two sides of our existence—that they are not as contradictory as you might have held them to be. It seems that some of you are now experiencing an opening to a new realm that includes these two sides of our humanness.

We have begun the discussion of human relationship because that is one of the most important contexts within which we experience and express the qualities of our Being. In our explorations here, relationship is usually seen as being between two. This can mean between two people, between two forces, or between our individual consciousness and God, true nature, or however we conceptualize what that "other" is.

We have begun the inquiry into the question of what it means to be a person in relationship to another person in a real way. The expression of divine eros emerges most explicitly within this context, although it is not limited to that. In fact, much of the teaching about divine eros was initiated and opened up by our experiences of the erotic nature of love in relation to the divine as the Beloved. For eros to be divine, we must express the embodiment of life and love as one. Having the capacity to be in the world in a way that does not separate us from spirit, while also feeling the pleasure of our energy, our erotic nature, our aliveness and love, makes life complete. We want to experience our humanness, but we don't want to divide ourselves to do it. We want to know more about both the spiritual and the worldly reality and how the two interrelate, because they are naturally a part of what it means to be human.

As a part of life and earthly existence, we also value relationships and are interested in being able to be with another in a way that expresses the preciousness of Being. But if we continue to relate in our usual patterns and habits, expecting to experience divine eros, we will find ourselves in an exercise of frustration. The marriage of heaven and earth is the experience of knowing who we are as being both beyond time and within the world. Our ordinary sense of self has no such capacity. Only the truth of our nature can encompass the transcendent and the immanent. This nature is what is real.

To be real means that we need to be able to live in a way that reflects the reality of what we truly are. It is important to recognize, however, that being real doesn't happen in a moment. Learning what it means to be a real person is a process of unfoldment and transformation. It is not something you fall into or recognize all of a sudden, as it sometimes can be in the discovery of or awakening to true nature. It is a maturational process. And it begins with being honest, truthful, and real about where you are and investigating that. Every moment holds the possibility of more realness and more in-touchness with the presence of essential Being.

We want to be human and we want to be real. Real humans are

magical creatures, but they are rare. In fact, we are magical creatures beyond our wildest imagination. Hameed once said, "We are actually elephants trying to be butterflies." And right after that, he said, "We are actually butterflies trying to be elephants." The first statement reflects our belief that our earthbound self is a heavy, solid mass rather than the luminous colorful beauty of the liberated lightness of Being that we long to be. The second describes our forgotten lightness, as we become a worldly creature and take a more substantial form. Sadly, both statements reflect the unsatisfying existence of most human beings.

Our actual situation is even stranger than that. We are not creatures of this world even though we live here. We are not born here and we don't die here. Being emerges into time and space, creating time and space as it emerges into and as this world. Being arises in forms, birthing itself into existence. One of those forms is the human one, that of you and me, and that form changes all throughout life until it is shed, perhaps for other forms.

Waves in an Ocean

We can see our nature as a vast ocean of consciousness. All manifestation arises out of that consciousness, and each of us is a unique wave in this vast ocean. However, our usual, temporal experience is akin to being a wave without an ocean, merely one object in a void, floating among other objects and separated from them by time and space. We take the surface appearance to be all there is, rather than as form that is arising within the vast ocean of consciousness. The problem is not the fact that we have come into this world, have been born into a body, and are living in the world of physicality. It is that we believe that the top of the ocean or the shape of the wave is the entire reality. Through our bodily senses, we experience the forms of this physical world. Through them, we come to believe that this world is the ground from which we originate, and that our existence is dependent on physical form and content.

Yet, from the realized point of view, all experiences, including the physical, are just waves in the ocean. From our limited view, spiritual experiences are miracles that come from some other, invisible dimension, but when we know the ocean—when we know reality directly and fully—we see how much more fundamentally real it is. This exposes the flimsiness of the ideas we have and reveals the truth that the individual consciousness is actually a personal expression of a vast ocean of reality. But to the person who is truncated from her essential ground, it seems like a miracle: "Oh, I had this opening . . . this amazing presence of light came, and I felt so wonderful . . ." We believe that it was an unusual event, that it was something other than what we are.

The wave can awaken to her wateriness and the source of her existence in a more complete way. Experiencing the light is one thing. To awaken to it and recognize it as true, and to know it as one's nature, is quite another. When the wave knows that the ocean is the source, this is realization. When the wave feels the ocean and experiences the wetness without knowing it and recognizing it, this is a spiritual experience that remains unexplainable, unknown, and unrealized. It is still part of the dream. It is not yet an awakening.

An example of the contrast between our usual view of reality and the view from a larger perspective can be described by borrowing an idea from the speculative novel *Flatland* by Edwin Abbott Abbott, published in 1884. It is an amazing and simple way to illustrate the perspectives of different dimensions that we don't usually think of. Let's say we live in a two-dimensional world. That world exists as a flat surface, so one can only move around on a single plane; there is no up and down, only back and forth, or side to side. Anything from the third dimension that comes into this two-dimensional reality would only be by implication, by virtue of the fact that something had manifested out of nowhere in the plane. Something appeared, but no explanation for it is totally satisfying, because much of the picture is not visible.

For example, a sphere moving through a two-dimensional plane would show itself first as a dot, then as a circle getting bigger and bigger and bigger, and then at some point, starting to get smaller and smaller and smaller. The last experience of it would be a point of contact where the sphere still touches the plane as it passes through. So we might think we've had a visitation from God: "Honey, I saw it again today. There was this thing that appeared, and it got bigger and bigger and then smaller and smaller . . . and then it was gone, just the way it came! It was an amazing presence rippling through." That would seem to be a miracle.

Zoom out: A little boy is playing with a ball and tosses it into the water. It hits the surface of the water, submerges, and then pops back out and the boy retrieves it. From a 3-D point of view, what has happened is all very explainable. From a 2-D perspective—along the surface of the water—it is a visitation from another dimension. Imagine waking up one day from your two-dimensional existence and discovering that you exist in three dimensions. You would realize, "Oh my God, there really is a sphere. It looks totally different than I thought. I never could have imagined . . . I thought a sphere did not feel like anything . . . but no, you can actually touch it. It's round and you can put your arms around it." You can grasp that that dimension is real, and this realization opens you up to a whole new realm of experience.

Your situation is like that, only more so. You are three-dimensional but much more. The other dimensions of our experience are beyond space and time, so the 3-D metaphor for the awakened condition is just that—only a metaphor. Recognizing what reality is and who we really are is much more mysterious than simply adding the experience of another spatial dimension.

When that wave loses touch with the vastness and depth of the ocean, we lose touch with the fullness and richness of Being. Then we don't know that we are a unique expression of the vastness. There is no other like you—you are completely unique; yet, at the depth, there is just one expressing itself as many. As the ocean, we are the nature of everything.

MIRACULOUS . . . OR SIMPLY REALITY?

We humans tend to believe in miracles instead of seeing that what we call a miracle is actually a glimpse into what is real. We distance ourselves from the miraculous by remaining in our conventional sense of who we are. We continue to be defined by our past experiences, so that what our parents believed and taught us and what we have learned about this world and the universe dominate and limit our experiences. Our minds pattern our world and keep it tightly circumscribed, limited to the most physical, sensate experiences. Parents, other family members, and teachers are forever present in our minds and always will be, as long as we relate to the world as they taught us to. They are part of a larger worldview and live on within it as part of us, limiting our freedom and restricting our perceptions from expanding. Even after these people have died, we are in constant relationship to them in our minds; they are still there, patterning our experience of ourselves.

Our images of them and our images of ourselves are mixed with feelings and sensations. This is all part of the patterned responses we come to know as relationship. Not only is our worldview patterned, our relationships are also patterned through the veils of past experiences and learning. We relate to others through this veil.

We also see and experience our body through the veils of the conventional. Our body defines our location, but we do not always experience it in the same way. When you have experiences of yourself in various conditions, you feel your body in different ways. Furthermore, your emotional or spiritual states often show you that something is happening that does not correspond with your *physical* body, but you do not always see the implications of your experience. For example, you can have experiences of being expansive—sometimes you even feel that your body is growing larger. You look down and say, "I feel like I'm out here beyond the physical boundaries . . . it's not my body exactly . . . what is it?" You are having the perception that there is some kind of sensitive field that can expand beyond your body, that has experiences that aren't the same shape as your body. Yet you continue to feel and act as though this body were all of what and who you are—even though you are having experiences to the contrary.

So you continue to define yourself by how you appear at the most superficial level, rather than taking those glimmers from beyond very personally and very seriously, in the sense that they mean something and are telling you something. The question is, what?

The sensitive field of the human being, which is a wave of the ocean of consciousness, is conscious beyond our physical body. We are a medium of aware and vibrant sensitivity, which is impressionable and usually patterned by our previous experiences. When we awaken to our nature, our experience changes. The new ways we experience ourselves challenge the old forms we have taken ourselves to be; we change into new forms and into formless realms of our nature as well.

Having a real relationship follows the same principle. It is an evolution of two waves of consciousness interacting and interweaving as one field of consciousness, shifting form through the interchange. This is the relational field as a living medium. What does it mean to have a real relationship? What does it mean to come together and not be defining your friend, partner, wife, by the experiences you had of them last week? What would it mean to actually see, with fresh eyes, who they are right now? This doesn't mean that you forget what has happened, who they are, or what their name is. It begins by taking the chance to open into the new, in the same way we do when we enter into our own experience and open that up.

Opening Up the Real Relationship

We are opening the field of consciousness and inviting it to reveal itself to us. We want to be able to suspend our idea of the relationship enough to invite in something new by opening to what's there right now. This means opening to things besides the color of a person's hair, the things he says, their interests, where she was born, what culture he is from. All of those are real in the sense that they are part of our experience in the world, but to invite our spiritual nature into the field means opening into other possibilities, new possibilities.

Growing up and maturing through the experiences the world has offered us has been important for our development. The next level of development involves starting out as a child in the spiritual world and maturing into adulthood by becoming a complete human being who knows her true nature and is nourished through it. In other words, the adult of this world is the child of the spiritual world. The adult of the spiritual world has a foot in both worlds and feels them as one. And real relating can only happen between two mature adults. The more mature we are, the more the relational field can open to new potential, and the less the past dictates the content of experience.

Our maturational process does not flourish if we disregard this world, push it away, or disown our parents. It is a matter of embracing everything and finding an opening to that other possibility, that next dimension of experience—the inner dimensions. Scientists say there are many physical dimensions that we don't know about. Who knows—perhaps this is the only way they can interpret the evidence they are finding. What is true, and what many of you actually know, is that our inner dimensions are rich and full, and that they are many and varied. By "inner," I don't mean only inside our bodies, I mean the inner nature of everything. Opening to the inner dimensions of experience is the completion of our maturational process.

When we are more complete as human beings and have matured into our depth, we become servants of that depth by living a life that is full and human, without ever leaving this transcendent depth. A relationship serves this depth in a similar way. In relationship we are more complete in the sense that we have recognized, realized, and integrated who we are. In maturing into our depth, we become transparent to the pure qualities of Being, and the aspects and deeper dimensions of experience come through in our relational expression.

When I say "real relationship," I mean one that is developing in an optimizing way, that enables those involved to become transparent to deeper truth and reality. Due to the interactive dynamic force in the relational field, the relationship becomes a field of consciousness that opens to new forms of experience. This means that we can continually become more real; we can continually learn and discover new aspects of ourselves, of the other, and of the potential of relationship. And we can live in a way that actually embodies those aspects, revealing more about them through our living and interacting.

"Complete" doesn't mean "finished." Completeness is a process; it is always completing. So how do we get there from where we are? We don't. We don't get anywhere. The process of maturing means that we nurture the seed that is here. We experience some human development, we come to some recognition of who we are, what we desire, what we long for. And we start with that. When we are speaking to another person, we start with where we are. We are as real as we can be; we recognize what we're feeling and we experience that as fully as we can. We do our best, without trying to manipulate ourselves or control our experience. This is actually a spiritual practice, which embodies all the principles of this work that we have discussed.

A real relationship is based on real relating, where each person is as present as possible, with the mutual intention to be open to one another. The more present and open we are, and the more we have real contact—true connection—the stronger the possibility of real relating will be. The less we define the other or ourselves through past experiences and personal history, the more our actions and responses will be based on what is present or needed in the moment, and the more the relationship will be an expression of the new revealing itself through the relational field. This means too that we need to see the other as a person who is a universe of experience, who has knowledge, wisdom, sensitivity, experience, and a set of skills unique to him or her.

We spend a lot of time in our conventional world assuming many things about people and not recognizing them as having their own uniqueness, much less appreciating that uniqueness. We try to adjust ourselves to what we think is needed or wanted, or we try to get someone else to adjust to us so that we get what we want, rather than suspending all of that for a moment and just having an interest in the other: "Who are you? I wonder how you feel. I wonder what matters to you. And I wonder why it matters in the way it does." Relating to one another without judgment, without trying to get someplace, but simply recognizing the universe of possibilities that is sitting in front of you. We are all the transcendent infinite ocean of Being and each an entire universe with its own qualities and characteristics. And the person appearing in front of you has his own flavor, his history, his likes and dislikes; his recognition of himself, his potential and his realization; his sensitivities and his presence. Right now, how he feels, how he experiences his life, how he experiences himself is different from how you experience yourself. Each individual is an entry into deeper knowing. And each experience of every individual is an opening. When you and another come together, the possibilities are multiplied exponentially through the two as one dynamic intermingling living field of consciousness.

When we relate to people only through our ideas about what we want and who we believe they are, it renders the relationship stagnant. Once you get to know somebody, that is just who they are. Little blips of newness may pop up here and there, but often we assume we know someone and then rigidify in our mind who we think they are. This reification of another not only limits our ability to continue knowing someone, but limits the relationship as well. There is a universe that neither of you can know yet, because it lies in the intermingling of your consciousnesses as the conduit for new awakenings. For the relational field to evolve, it is necessary to consider the person we are with in a way that allows the energetic field of consciousness to open up and be illuminated with the light of spirit. When this occurs in a conscious way, relationship is infused with the divine and is very much on earth at the same time.

The more we open up, both to ourselves and to the other, and the more the field opens us up to the new and the now, the more we realize that there is much that is yet to be revealed. When I see students opening to a new discovery, I frequently hear them say, "Oh my God, I had no idea . . ." and I can see the recognition dawning . . . so much more is there than one could ever imagine. The mystery feels palpable, and the process of discovery is further invigorated.

How I see it is that to be a complete human being means that we are in a process of continually opening and learning more and more about the universe within, and this process continues in our relational experience with others. We learn about the other and ourselves in the interaction and, even more than that, new universes are created by that unique relationship. No two are alike. Like two galaxies colliding and spinning out new patterns painted with stardust, we can enhance and bring out parts of this universe that wouldn't be touched or manifest otherwise.

Realization is a very alone kind of process, where inner aloneness is necessary to realize our true being. Realization adds to the field in terms of knowing Being as your nature and not depending on the other for that knowing. A profound ground for a relationship is created when there are two who know themselves in this way. It also works in reverse: The two can discover their nature through the relationship. This is more rare but definitely possible, if we are truly open to learning, because in the relational field, interaction brings out parts of us that don't come out easily any other way. The relational field opens up the possibilities of our personal expression a thousandfold, allowing the arising and the understanding of our reactions and emotional patterns, the things we enjoy and delight in, the spiritual qualities of our nature, and so on. These potentials open the field further, and they continue to unfold indefinitely as we keep learning more through our interactions—not just with significant others, but in our daily interactions with many people.

This type of opening that can develop with one particular person, perhaps a mate or a very close friend with whom we experience an exciting and dynamic relational quality, can become a unitive conduit for realization which is of a different order than just two people relating deeply. The relationship becomes a context in which we grow and learn, open and develop, where we feel a mutual interest in each other's well-being. When a love relationship or a marriage is working, the openness becomes a ground for growing and maturing, at the same time furthering the realization of the universe.

EMPATHY FOR THE OTHER

Often, the needs and tasks of daily life eclipse the openness, love, and creative involvement—but they don't have to. Unstructured space and time is necessary for the maturation of a relationship. This allows us to slow down and take our attention off worldly concerns and go inward together. We also need certain qualities that allow the field to open and evolve. For example, it is necessary to have some sensitivity to where the other is. We need a sense of empathy in concert with an interest in what the other is feeling, rather than assuming we know where he or she is coming from. We can get to know where our partner is not only by external cues but by actually feeling it.

Empathy is generally seen as the ability to know another's point of view, the ability to relate to what your friend is saying, feeling, or thinking because you have had the experience and can call it up in your memory. It stimulates the sense of knowing from your own experience, which you can then apply to how another person might be feeling. But empathy can go very, very deep, much deeper than this psychological way of knowing the other's experience. We can actually *feel* where someone is without having had their experience, because our consciousness is ultimately one ocean. A wave in the ocean is not separate from the other waves. We can feel the waves of others and the particular states of those around us as our sensitivity develops. It has been confirmed through neuroscientific experiments that with empathy we can actually experience another person's pain through the activity of mirroring neurons. Here, we are discussing empathy in a larger sphere, as including all states and feelings of the other, not just their pain.

When a relationship has gone stale, there is often a loss of sensi-

tivity and empathy. Your husband comes home, and you're crying
. . . you've had a terrible day . . . and he says, "Hi, honey, what's for
dinner?" You're incredulous that he shows no interest, has no sense
of what is going on with you: "What? You see me like this and that's
the first thing you're asking me? My father just died. I feel devas-
tated." There is no empathy, no attunement. The response isn't attuned to where you are. This can be quite painful and will usually
not lead to opening to the other.

Attunement is a way we use empathic sensitivity; it is an action
based on sensitivity to another such that your response matches
what is happening with her. You get a sense of where she is coming
from and are able to respond in a way that speaks to that. For a relationship to evolve, for the relational field to open up and evolve, we
have to first really understand that there is a person, here too, with
her own feelings, her own experience. The more present we are, the
more real we are, and the more our heart is open and available, the
more this sensitivity of our consciousness is able to feel where someone is. And it is possible that our individual consciousness can get so
sensitive that we actually feel in ourselves what another person is
experiencing, in its totality and specifics.

How often have you walked into a room and immediately said
to yourself, "Hmm, it feels tense in here"? Then you find out that
somebody there is going through a hard time and you're picking up
on it. Or you feel uplifted the minute you walk in—"Oh, it feels really nice in here"—and you find out that something joyful has been
going on in the house. We don't have to actually see somebody and
get physical cues to feel what is happening. Our consciousness is sensitive. Our humanness has a sensitivity to it beyond the nervous sys-
tem. It is more of a gut feeling at first, but it can manifest as an actual
set of sensations corresponding to specific emotions and spiritual
states of consciousness.

Empathy is an extremely important characteristic for us to have
in order to open up the relational field and support it to develop.
When we are in relation to another, the limitations of our empathy,
sensitivity, and attunement will limit how much that field will

open. If we believe that we know a person as much as he can be known, we have closed the book on him. And it is not unusual that we come to merely serve a function for one another after a while. The other becomes some sort of thing that has a useful place in your life: You get up, and your breakfast is already on the table. You down it hurriedly, tossing off your thanks, and your wife says, "That's what I'm here for." You run out the door saying, "Great, see you later; I'm off to work"—and she thinks, "Great, that's what *you're* here for."

There is no longer a development of anything new. Everything is simply about maintaining familiar roles. Being together might even be pleasant, but it's not alive. Maybe there is nothing bad about this—it works and we do need to have agreements and a division of labor in our relationships. But not at the expense of the relationship itself. We all have roles we fulfill for one another, but the relationship becomes empty after a while if that's all there is. If we are only with each other for what is useful, eros goes to sleep, saying, "Come back later when you've freshened up!"

The excitement and thrill of eros are important for nurturing the aliveness of a relationship. This aliveness is what enables the relational field to continue to open, to grow, to develop and renew. Through the support and sensitivity of empathic attunement, two individuals not only grow within the relationship but also become more united as one living field.

MUTUALITY IN THE FIELD

In addition to sensitivity and empathy, to openness and interest, there needs to be a measure of mutuality. A relationship does not open up if it is not mutual, if one person is interested while the other isn't. Mutuality means that two people have a similar degree of interest in one another. If someone has less interest, then a dissonance or disharmony will result that will limit the relationship's potential. One person wants more than the other is willing to give, and it becomes a push-pull situation. For the relational field to open up, mutual curiosity about the other is important—two people who can see one another as having an inner life that is distinct, unique, and interesting. Then two galaxies can come together and create one field that has an interactive synergy.

The relational field develops by two fields of consciousness coming together through an interaction in which the two fields become part of one relational field. In fact, sometimes the two fields become simply the one field opening up. When we talk about the relational field, we are talking about a field of consciousness that is participatory on the part of two or more individuals. As we sit in this room together, we are in a field of consciousness; the group field is gaining more presence as we focus on this topic. The group presence is a support for our work. We each add something to it. And every group is different in quality due to the various mix of individuals that comprise it.

When we are interacting with another person, one of the possibilities is that we create this synergistic effect. We call it "looping" when the energy of the field is mutually enhancing in a kind of feedback loop where particular qualities in the field grow as the two impact one another in a mutual way. We can create a feedback loop that supports either shutting down or opening up the field. We are emphasizing the optimization of the field. You are probably not interested in learning how to close down.

The interactive field can look like this: You meet a friend and she says, "Hi, how are you doing today?"

If you are being honest, you might say, "I'm feeling kind of contracted and uncomfortable."

"Did something happen?"

"Well, actually, I had an interaction with someone that left me feeling upset . . ." And you start telling your story, but in a way that has truthfulness to it, with an interest in seeing what is there, rather than trying to avoid where you are. The relationship is centered on the truth, with a mutual interest in being authentic. So you continue, "You know, I'm feeling an opening as I'm telling you about this; I feel really good that I can talk to you. I'm feeling a kind of bubbliness or happiness about it . . . but there's also some tenderness."

"Yeah, I get that; it seems like something really touched you."

"My roommate was very harsh with me because I left the place messy, and I felt kind of bad about that. I went off to the workshop and she wasn't very happy to see me go without cleaning up. I didn't feel very supported."

"Wow, that's difficult."

"But I feel something is happening for me now . . . and I feel some sort of presence happening . . . actually, I'm surprised."

"Yeah, I'm feeling connected with you, a tender sort of presence that feels good to me. I really need that right now."

As you both continue to experience a kind of presence, it can build to the point where an expansion may occur:

"It's interesting . . . I feel like the entire story of this morning—my roommate and feeling bad about myself—is kind of left behind. It's not present here with you. Now I feel contactful and I'm interested in you. What made you ask how I was doing? Where did that come from?"

So there is a mutual interest in what's happening right now between you, along with the opportunity to open that up and let it develop. Just like in an individual inquiry, the development of the field can touch many areas, such as emotional content, mental ideas, and physical sensations, but in this case, the inquiry is into a shared field. However, there has to be an interest, a "want to know," and a sense of goodwill toward the other, even if something is bothering you about the person. And there needs to be a curiosity and interest in discovery. The spirit of discovery is important, and the curiosity needs to extend to finding out whatever may be bothersome or difficult in the interaction or in the other person. The interest in discovery becomes an adventure of discovery.

Eros requires that you give yourself the opportunity to be more real in your friendships, to allow them the space to open up to what they are and to what they can be. If you are feeling bothered when you are with somebody, you might find yourself saying, "Something about you reminded me of my husband, who wasn't very happy about my coming to the workshop this morning. And now I get that what I'm feeling is not about you." And as soon as you say this, you feel that a clearing can occur.

Your friend then says, "Wow, what was it like to have me sitting there, and you're thinking that I'm your husband?"

"It's kind of odd . . . when I first saw you, I actually thought that you look like him, but now I see that you don't at all. Now you look like my mother, and I like my mother! So now it feels good . . . but I realize the good feeling is something I'm feeling with you now; it's not because you remind me of her. It isn't about my mother at all, but it is the same good feeling I have with her . . ." The field between you and your friend can open up in many, many ways.

You can feel the presence between you, and the presence can bring more consciousness to what is happening—and that, in turn, can bring out excitement or more wanting to know. The other person can start to feel the excitement, and his responsiveness can become more and more attuned because you are getting more and more where he is, rather than remaining stuck in your ideas about him and your notions of what you want from him. What is happening is that you are getting more in touch with your own presence. You are not trying to become a fuller wave by connecting with the other and thinking that the ocean is in that person. You are connecting to the ocean through being more fully yourself in the interaction. Being present in the interaction supports presence to come more into the foreground for you and the other person, and it supports the field to deepen and expand. Our practice, then, is to stay true to what is going on, to remain grounded in where we are, and keep in touch with our intention to focus inward.

EXPLORATION SESSION

This particular inquiry practice will be done in three parts with another person.

1. Each of you will spend ten minutes doing a solo inquiry, starting with finding out where you are in the moment and letting that open up in whatever way it does.

A lot has probably come up for you already, which gives you a chance to dip into your own recognition of what is happening for you and let that open up and deepen. Allow yourself to suspend the idea that you already know where you are. You have some experiences about where you are; you have some sensations; you might be in touch with some reactions; and you might be in touch with some presence. That is where you begin your inquiry. You don't want to displace your ideas and beliefs and pretend you don't know anything. You want to take all of your experiences into consideration but suspend the belief that these are all there is to you.

Allow yourself to be interested in sensing where you are, feeling into it, letting your ideas, feelings, and sensations be there. But also question, wonder, think about where you are in ways you haven't let yourself before. "Why am I feeling this way? What happened, exactly, that brought this about?" Or "I'm feeling this presence—what is it exactly? What does it feel like? What does it mean?" Let yourself allow whatever is arising to open up . . . let the dynamism itself show you the next step.

If you attend with interest and curiosity to where you are—whether it's a reaction or new arising—typically something will bubble up: "Oh, this reminds me of . . ." Or maybe it brings in a certain attitude: "I've been feeling this way for a week now. Actually, this started before I even got here. What's happening is just making it more obvious to me." And then some sense of what your experience is about might arise. Or perhaps you will feel some resistance: "No, I don't want to go here right now; I want to have the relational experience; that's what I want to feel."

Okay, let yourself feel what you want and what you don't want, but be clear about what your feeling is and let yourself go into it: "I don't want to feel this—but what will happen if I do?" Let yourself meet yourself on the road to going inward and find out what is there.

2. Move into a dialectic inquiry together, into the field of expe-

rience that you and your partner will be having together. You both want to see what is in the field you share, to consider how it feels, to notice what the experience is like between you. Take twenty-five minutes to do this part.

The dialectic inquiry might begin with talking about how you are feeling with one another after hearing what the other person had to say. Start there and see what develops. As you are speaking, something in particular might begin to happen that you can feel in the space between you.

Or perhaps you will just feel the presence in the field. You can start by acknowledging that rather than by engaging first thing in a dialogue. Whatever happens, you want to pay attention to what the relational field feels like as you are engaged with each other. Just explore it; be experimental. Let yourself take risks, but keep sensing. See if you can actually feel what is happening between you, rather than just having an intellectual understanding of where your partner is.

Remember that dialectic inquiry is an interactive inquiry. You are not simply discussing your experience together, but rather you are also expressing yourself and responding to the expressions of the other. Expressions will need to be appropriate and responsive, and avoid attacks, judgments, criticisms, therapizing each other, or reading each other psychically. It is a mutual cooperative endeavor, a collaborative relational adventure in the discovery of reality.

3. After the dialectic inquiry, have a discussion by reflecting on the dialectic exercise. You want to see how sensitive your empathy was in the dialectic. When your partner was talking about where she was, what was your experience? You want to see how much empathy was there. How were you experiencing the empathy, the attunement? Was there a responsiveness that felt attuned or were you feeling "off" with each other and not really getting where each other was? See how empathy, sensitivity, and attunement functioned in the field and how they were being expressed there.

You want to discover what a sensitive relational field is in your personal experience and how the relational field can liberate the loving, alive, erotic presence of the divine. Keep in mind that this can happen between friends, between lovers, between any two people, because any relational field has these particular characteristics. So give it a go.

QUESTIONS AND COMMENTS

Student: You were saying that it is sometimes easier to be more open with friends than with partners. I just tried to do the exercise with my husband; we are twenty-three years together now. We just realized how difficult it is to not come from our well-known patterns of communicating with each other. Our history comes in, our projections and expectations, and so on. I wonder what your experience is . . . how to bring more of this quality of being present now into the relationship with a partner? What would be helpful? What could open it up more?

Karen: In my experience, recognizing that you are in a pattern is the first step. Becoming articulate about that in the moment is the next one: "I realize now that I'm in the same pattern I usually fall into . . . I'm finding that I'm becoming this kind of person, and it feels this way to me . . ." These patterns are typically accompanied by a bodily sensation; it is not just that you are saying the same things that you always do. So it is good to see what the body can contribute. Notice its sensations, energy, posture, and movement.

Student: It was very helpful for me to keep asking myself, "What is now, what is in this moment, what do I feel with you now?"—but the old patterns are so automatic.

Karen: When you asked yourself, "What do I feel with you now?" what happened?

Student: I felt a lot of openness in the moment and also an openness to really meet, and to speak out all the time—"I want to meet you now."

Karen: Did you tell him that?

Student: Yes.

Karen: Did something happen?

Student: It opened more with me. It opened something between us. There were moments where it was really the now. It felt so immediate compared to how it feels when we're in the patterns that have developed in our history together.

Karen: Having those glimpses will open up the pattern, and you may see that there is even more possibility. What happened shows you that you need to be able to do that more. Find the time to sit together.

Student: I get very curious.

Karen: Feel the curiosity. What happens in you when you feel curious?

Student: I get excited about it. There is really more to him.

Karen: And how do you feel about him?

Student: Good. It tastes good. I have a feeling that there is much to discover.

Karen: And what you are showing us right now is that you felt the pattern and the openness. They can both be there. You don't have to throw away the pattern or try to distance yourself from it. You can see that there is openness within the pattern, too, and that will help to evolve it, open it up, and bring things out.

Student: I felt that very strongly—that both are there.

Karen: It is important to not just look at the pattern and say, "How can I get rid of this?" There is information in the pattern that is important to understand. If you are open to one another, and you are curious and there is a lot to discover, then the history of how you've been in relationship can give you information about how you see yourself and how you see him. And you can open that up into a whole new world. You can use the pattern, with the openness, to discover and let that be a kind of an inner dialectic. Your relationship can become an adventure.

Student: Thank you.

Karen: It's exciting.

Student: Since this morning, during the meditation, I had a strong feeling that my friend is here as well, but she died four years ago. It's strange to have her here. I am a little bit confused about whether I can be present when she is here. Now I don't know what to do, because it scares me as well, and I'm feeling quite tense.

Karen: When you say she is here, how do you experience her?

Student: Well, it's more the sadness; I have fantasies of what I would do with her if she were here. It is this strong desire to touch her, to show her what I'm doing, to let her see all the things that life brings now. She was my playmate once.

Karen: Let yourself feel the desire to connect with her and show her all that you are now, and just see what happens. And also feel the sadness that she is not here to share with you. Take a few breaths.

Student: I feel that when she died, we were so open; that is a little bit what I'm feeling this week—that everything is coming open. But I feel unsafe with it. I feel a kind of risk because I feel I can lose it any minute and I told the person with whom I did the inquiry. I'm not sure if I was honest, because I am kind of scared.

Karen: Let yourself feel scared and feel what you need. What do you feel you need in order to feel safe?

Student: Actually, I feel safe. I thought my friend had to go. I thought that I couldn't be present in the inquiry when she is there also, so I wanted her to leave. But she didn't go. And now it feels like it can all be here.

Karen: Why did you feel that you didn't want her to be here?

Student: I didn't think that it was respectful to the other person in the inquiry. I felt distracted.

Karen: What is the presence you feel at the moment? Is there something you are experiencing that is making you feel safer right now?

Student: I think it is important to feel deeper about the sadness. It is the safe area inside.

Karen: What does that safe place inside feel like?

Student: Warm. New, but also alone.

Karen: What kind of warm?

Student: It feels like the warmth that I lost.

Karen: Interesting!

Student: I think I was scared, and now it's the same thing—I am scared, I think. Now the warmth is there, but it is really strange to stay in the moment because I'm scared to lose it—that's the point.

Karen: That is a very good point. Sometimes when we are in touch with something—like right now that warmth feels very, very real, and it feels safe and it feels holding and there is a good feeling—but you are afraid of being disconnected again from that and feeling the pain of that disconnection. For you, it will be like losing your friend again.

Student: Yeah, yeah . . .

Karen: That is the risk we take. It's true. But let it be there and just see what happens. It seems your friend represented safety.

Student: Absolutely she did.

Karen: So it seems that whether her presence was actually here or it was an idea of her being here, it's irrelevant. You needed to feel in yourself the safety that she represented for you, in a way that feels really true. And by longing for it, letting yourself feel the loss of it, you reconnected to it.

Student: Yeah.

Karen: Thank you—that was a very beautiful illustration of the possibilities in relationships where the object of our love is not actually here but rather in our mind. It is important to invite the feeling or the presence of the person because sometimes these things that arise within us have meaning for what is coming up now in our lives. Sometimes when we open, fear comes. We have images and ideas about others that we have known or know now. But sometimes it is as if we feel their presence. You just felt it as somebody else appearing in your consciousness, somebody you love and miss. This is an interesting possibility for relationships, which has many degrees of subtlety and variation of experiencing the other's presence. For some of us, it happens in a different way: We transfer important people from the past onto the one we are talking to now. We need to allow that and say, "You remind me of . . ." or "I'm missing my friend right now. I really need her to be here, but I feel like she shouldn't be, because we are talking." Bring it in and let yourself have that truth in the inquiry. You don't have to exclude anything.

Student: For me it was interesting because I was attracted to my new friend from Israel and I wasn't sure about asking him to do the exercise. He is from Israel and I am a German and there was this common history we have to carry. I was immediately present with my history, feeling the sadness, the sorrow, and the guilt. I took it on when I was a child, because my father had this guilt and couldn't deal with it. I tried to take it, but I couldn't handle it; it wasn't possible.

I spent time in Israel, and when I was there I was a lot in contact with seeing the effects of the Holocaust. And my soul was not able to handle the pain. But here I was sitting in front of somebody who didn't have an object relation with me as a German, so I could open more to the pain. It gave me support.

Karen: And what happened between you then?

Student: It changed into a very intimate contact.

Karen: So there was openness to what was. Some sort of intimacy could happen.

Student: It was incredible.

Karen: So your history became something that was not between you.

Student: There was no history in the experience, after a while; there was just openness and no history at all. There was nothing in between.

Karen: Beautiful . . . hope for humanity.

Student: In the dialectic inquiry, I found myself very aware of very short distances between one bit of content and another. I tend to lose myself, or my awareness or presence, in the very short space between. When we talked about something and then felt somehow it is finished, I got sad. I felt a kind of gap. We saw something in each other's eyes, and it could last forever, and then suddenly this gap arose—what is here now?

Karen: You got scared?

Student: Yes, scared about what she would think about me when I look at her for so long and she doesn't say anything. There was some restlessness then, and me feeling I have to say something. But I turned inward—how do I feel right now? what do I sense right now?—just to bring something into communication. This has a kind of force, which I don't like. I would rather like to look in her eyes. When I feel this kind of force happening, this is where I tend to lose my awareness or I get trapped into finding content.

Karen: It sounds like you got self-conscious and a little frightened. Do you know what scared you about looking? Was there anything that came up?

Student: Nothing specific . . . unknown, unexpected things will maybe come up, and maybe there would be a need to protect myself.

Karen: That would be something you could say: "I'm scared right now and I'm concerned that I'm looking in your eyes too much."

Student: I told her.

Karen: And what happened?

Student: We were both very open and very relaxed and we also shared that, but I was very aware of these small moments where I felt the way I just told you. Usually in relationship I don't feel this . . . instead I get out of the relationship because we don't have the time— and before I can feel the moments of disconnection. Here the time is set . . . we stay in contact for twenty-five minutes, so I feel the gaps. These small moments are a possibility for me to go out of the contact, not only with the person but also with myself.

Karen: If I understand, it's that you don't like it when that comes up; you want to be able to remain in contact.

Student: I feel it's a pattern to go out of contact, to be with myself and not be in this thrilling contact, where nobody knows where it will lead.

Karen: That is part of the process; these things come up and you get the chance to let them come before you so you have the opportunity to understand them, see through them. That can open up to something else, and each time something comes forward, you can learn more about what makes it come up for you. We can feel the fear of being too intimate or the fear of someone going away. These are important to notice. It is part of the process of being clarified. It's like clouds in the sky evaporating . . . and then we see the sky itself. The past may arise and cloud the view.

All of these things are opportunities, although we feel them as "I don't want it to wreck the openness." Actually, letting them come up is part of what the openness is doing. It is inviting more of you, including the parts that are frightened, the historical parts, the fear, the sadness . . . all kinds of things can come and be in the way of real contact. But if we allow them, we will see more about them, and then the sky becomes even clearer. This kind of unfoldment, it seems, was happening with you.

Student: I am very grateful for these opportunities to have these dialectical inquiries.

Karen: And the openness can lead us into deeper and deeper openness that lets us get more and more in touch with ourselves and more in touch with the other. This gives rise to intimacy, which is the feeling that we are in touch with ourselves and we're really honoring where someone else is, without being blended so that we are a puddle. In fact, there is a field of depth and appreciation, and that's when the openness takes us deeper into the presence of what's there.

Music Meditation

Suggested Selection:

The aria "Ebben? Ne andrò lontana" from act 1 of Alfredo Catalani's opera *La Wally* (sung by Wilhelmenia Wiggins Fernandez on the soundtrack CD of the movie *Diva*)

Let's end this section with a music meditation that speaks to this kind of depth that is possible in human relationships. After you have put on the music and settled in comfortably, take a deep breath and sense into your body, particularly your belly. You may be feeling disconnected from others. Just be aware of that. You may feel desirous of a connection. You might be feeling some level of depth in yourself but not with another. You might be feeling the depth of intimacy with another. Wherever you are is fine. Intimacy is a possibility we have with our inner beloved or outer beloved, in our friendships, marriages, and contacts. Let's allow ourselves to feel the depth of whatever level of openness, contact, and intimacy we are experiencing. Just let it open and take you further.

7

Sexual Love

HAMEED

WE WILL AGAIN CHANT the secret name of divinity—HU. As we do our chant this time (see p. 51), we still feel it coming from the belly, but we also feel it in the heart with a sense of closeness, a sense of intimacy, a sense of being very near to what we love more than anything else. Intimacy is a sense of soft, deep, profound closeness to ourselves, to what is precious and real in us. As we hear the chanting all around us, we feel this intimacy pervading the whole space. We are not only intimate inside; the heart is outside as well. We are in the heart and the heart is in us as we feel the intimacy with our inner Beloved, who is also the surround. When the chant is finished, we will continue sitting with the Kath meditation (see p. 9).

DEVELOPING RELATIONSHIP

You have probably noticed that we have taken somewhat of a detour in our exploration of divine eros. It becomes important for our inquiry into divine eros to also inquire into relationships. That is why we have spent the time learning something about true or real relationship—what it is and how we can open it up so that it develops and becomes even more real. In this teaching, real relationship both expresses our spiritual nature and helps us be more open to it. That is what "real" means. It doesn't mean that if I'm mad at my wife, I tell her I'm mad. This feeling can be true, and expressing it can be authentic, but that is not what being real is. For us, it is only the beginning. Many people think that if you feel and express your feelings, you are being real. We need to be able to do that, but more than anything else, being real means that we can experience and express our spiritual nature.

In this understanding, true relationship supports both people to access their spiritual nature more easily, and it is also a place to express it, to live it. You can definitely express your spiritual nature freely with your dog or your parrot. But it is more satisfying to express it with another human being, in the sense that what you express will be more complete, more total. And it can be reciprocated in kind.

We are exploring the practice of dialectic inquiry while learning the practice of inquiry in general. We have seen that we can communicate with another person in a way that opens both of us more deeply to ourselves and each other. Then the relationship itself can expand and deepen the discovery of each of us, our relationship, and reality as a whole. In other words, a true relationship is one that helps us to discover reality. It's fine if a relationship doesn't help us do that—most human relationships are this way—but that is not what we are learning here. We are exploring how to develop relationship in new and unimagined ways.

To do this, we need to develop certain interactive skills, what we call relational skills. We have discussed and explored a number of these, including the role of being personal, being open, and making direct and immediate contact, as well as the importance of feeling connected and having sensitivity for ourselves and for each other. As we have seen, being sensitive means having a delicate awareness, a very attuned awareness. Relational sensitivity includes empathy, being able to sense where the other person is coming from, what is happening with him or with her. It also includes attunement, which is the capacity to respond and relate in a way that considers where another person is. We don't just express ourselves, we express ourselves to that particular person at that particular time. If we are not attuned, our friend will not completely get the communication.

A real relationship is, by definition, open, which means that it is open to further developments. When a relationship is open and real, we have a better opportunity to discover deeper dimensions of reality, sometimes more powerfully than just when we are by ourselves. This is one reason why having a teacher is more powerful than working by oneself. A relationship with another person—whether in a friendship, an intimate relationship, or a marriage—can be powerful for our inner journey if it is real and open to new possibilities. An energizing dynamic can occur when two forces are interacting with each other—two souls, two vortexes of consciousness, blending their energies together. You are not simply adding one to the other—it's not like one plus one equals two. It is more powerful than that. This is due to what we call mutuality, where there is not only interaction but also mutual interest—a common interest in the truth and a mutual desire to know one another. This shared interest in the discovery of the truth becomes a mutual love for discovering each other at the same time as we discover ourselves.

When you combine mutuality with empathy and attunement, a very powerful dynamic results, which we experience as a mutual impact, a mutual influence. As I communicate or express myself to my friend, this does something to her. The communication doesn't just give her information, it affects her consciousness, it changes her state. And seeing how my communication affects her affects me. So the necessary openness includes an openness to seeing that what I say and what I do have an impact, an influence, on the other person. It affects her emotionally, it affects her consciousness, it affects her state, but I am also open to being affected by her. I am open for her communication to impact me, to influence me. When there is mutual openness, then mutual influence can create a feedback loop.

For example, I say, "I am sorry I criticized you; I see that it hurt you." My partner recognizes my sorrow and she feels gratitude. As I see that she feels gratitude, my tears flow and I feel my love for her. Seeing my love for her opens her love for me. And because we have empathy, I not only see that she loves me, I also feel her love. As I feel her love, it increases my love. And my deepened and expanded love deepens and expands hers. It keeps going like that, in a spiral of deepening and expanding relating. That is what is meant by a feedback loop. It is fed by an openness to mutual influence.

Most people experience this feedback loop in a negative way when they are fighting. When they are angry at each other, yelling and screaming and calling each other names, things frequently spiral out of control and become explosive. But the feedback loop can also be of love, mutual enjoyment, mutual appreciation. All states can go deeper, expand, and become more powerful because of this dynamic of mutual impact. But we need to be open to it.

It is possible to reach the point where we are not afraid of being affected or impacted by our friend or our partner. Not only aren't we afraid, we feel we are strong enough, independent enough, to be affected by the other without feeling "I am going to lose myself." We actually welcome being impacted because we understand that being affected is a natural part of relationship. A relationship cannot be real if the people do not affect each other. When there is empathy in the interaction in addition to presence, then mutual impact, mutual influence, can expand the relationship to an amazing depth and intensity.

We understand how a relationship can be important for discovery, for inquiry, for learning about oneself and reality, but a relationship is not always needed for those things. Spiritual practice, most of the time, is solo practice. You meditate by yourself or inquire on your own. Even when you are on retreat with other people, you are meditating by yourself. But interacting as we have described it can create a forceful, powerful dynamic. We are usually afraid of this dynamic because we think it will spiral out of control emotionally and energetically. What would happen then? We could both get angry and that might lead to violence. We may even be afraid that we will feel too much pleasure or that if we lose control, we are both going to be scared. Have you noticed that when you are with somebody who is scared, you start feeling scared, too, and you have to calm them down; otherwise, you get more scared. That is why, if you want to see a scary movie, it is better to go to the theater—because everybody is scared. You feel more thrill, more intensity. If you watch the movie by yourself at home, it can also be scary but it is not as exciting. And if you get too scared, then you have to turn off the TV. If you are in a theater and you're scared, everybody else is scared, too, so that just makes it more exciting; you get to experience the thrill of that type of feedback.

When it is part of a true relationship, inquiry brings out our experience of vulnerability and openness, which tends to bring our true nature, the depth of who we are, into the interaction. At the depth of who we are, there are beautiful qualities: kindness, sweetness, appreciation, gratitude, clarity, brightness, depth, peacefulness, energy, dynamism, power, and so on. Imagine a dynamic in which both of you have a degree of empathy and are open to feel and be affected by each other, and where the relational field includes enjoyment of one another. You are enjoying the other person, you are just enjoying who he is. And if he is sensitive to you, he begins to feel your joy and begins to laugh with you, to become happy with you. That makes you enjoy him even more . . . and the interaction keeps deepening and expanding. After a while you can't stop laughing together, giggling, bubbling.

The interaction becomes much more intense, of course, when you're not only feeling the other's feelings and responding but you are also having strong feelings *toward* one another. That is why, for instance, you can be angry with someone and your wife will say, "I'm angry with him, too," and the two of you can be angry at him together. But being angry *at* each other is a lot more intense, because then it is very personal between you, which gives the feelings more power. It is the same when you are feeling love for one another. If you feel that you love the other person and the other person loves you, the intensity begins to loop. Then the love can develop and expand to include deeper qualities, such as sweetness, juiciness, and a nectar-like quality, with a delightful appreciation.

THE MANY FACES OF EROS

What happens if you throw desire into the mix? Then you not only love each other, you want each other—which is usually experienced sexually: "I don't just love you, I also find you quite yummy, very attractive. I am laying my eyes on you right now, but I would love to lay my hands on you!" And the other person says, "I was just feeling the same thing." We have all had experiences like that. Desire in itself is a powerful force. It is an energetic, instinctual primal force. As we have seen, desire is an expression of the powerful dynamism and energy of our Being. It is an expression of the creative force of the divine. And when desire is an expression of mutual love, it becomes an intensifying eruption. The interactive field between two people not only becomes charged up, it begins to sparkle, to throb, to pulsate. That is what desire brings to the field—a pulsation, a throbbing, an energetic quality. Your experience of immediacy feels not only sweet and appreciative but also like a throbbing, pulsating force that wants to move toward, wants to get closer to the other person. This is divine eros!

Most people don't consider the connection between the erotic and the divine aspects of the human being, because they conflate the erotic with the purely sexual. We saw the need for people to understand the potential of bringing these two sides of our humanness together, for seeing the hidden connection between them.

In the Diamond Approach, we differentiate between the erotic, the sexual, and the divine erotic. Eros is an expression of our basic life force, arising from the pelvis and belly center and experienced as a pulsating, throbbing, sensual vitality. Normally we experience erotic energy as sexual, but it need not be. You can be turned on by someone or something without being genitally aroused. So erotic relationship is a larger category of relationship that includes the sexual. In this teaching we have been exploring divine eros, which is when the erotic force, the dynamism of passion and desire, is combined with the selfless love of our heart. This combination reveals more of the full potential of eros, the life force, as an expression of our true nature. As with the erotic, the divine erotic can be sexual or not. Though sexual relationships are always erotic, they are not always an expression of divine eros, for there can be sex without love or an inner sense of presence, and divine eros always includes love. More specifically, divine eros requires the presence of selfless love, which is unusual in relationships of any kind.

So we are saying that a loving relationship can be erotic without being sexual. A friendship can be erotic in this way, for example, when love includes the interest and desire to be together, to enjoy each other, to delight in each other's presence and expressions. There is an erotic energy, a living, pulsating energy, in the interaction that makes the relationship dynamic and fun, playful and powerful in its disclosing of reality. Two people are turned on together to reality and turned on to each other's excitement about the discovery of reality. The dialectic inquiry will then have an erotic dimension that is full of pleasure and mirth, enjoyment and excitement, without it being physical or sexual.

This is a type of relationship that society does not acknowledge clearly, even though many people experience erotic energy in some of their loving connections with others. We tend to think of eros as always being sexual because conventional understanding cannot differentiate the erotic (or the divine erotic) from the sexually erotic. The result is that people repress the living force of eros in most relationships in order for those relationships to fit the conventions of friendship or family. Or if they feel the eros in the relationship, they believe they must express it sexually, with all its potential complications, for they cannot imagine eros being other than sexual energy.

One way divine eros expresses itself is the desire for intimacy— a loving desire to be intimate, close, to be as much in contact and in communication as possible. Love tends to bring out this type of desire. When we love somebody, we want to be intimate with that person; the movement toward intimacy is natural. We enjoy and we like being with him or her. It is natural for there to be dynamism, a flow toward being close and intimate, and to express the love together.

And this intimacy can go a step further. Let's consider the situation in which an erotic relationship includes both the divine and the sexual dimensions. Here, desire within the love relationship is for sexual intimacy, and eros becomes explicitly sexual: "I want to be close and intimate, but I also want to interact physically. And I want to interact physically in a very particular way. We may start with a hug, but that is only the beginning. And I don't want to just wrestle!" Sexuality adds another dimension to the interaction. One wants to express pleasure in the other person in a physically intimate way. There is a desire to experience pleasure together, giving pleasure and receiving pleasure in return, but including the body in addition to all that we have described divine eros to be.

Divine eros has inherent in it a selfless love; the desire is not just to experience pleasure, it is also to give pleasure. When you love somebody, you want her to feel good, you want her to be happy, you want her to experience enjoyment, happiness, satisfaction. In divine eros, experiencing satisfaction is also giving satisfaction. And by giving satisfaction, we experience satisfaction. The love is so dynamic that there is no difference between giving and taking, between love and desire. This is what true divine love means.

This giving and receiving of pleasure can happen in all relationships. When you love someone, you always have some desire for the other to have a good time and to be happy. In the intimacy of a love partnership, however, the erotic usually becomes more explicitly sexual. This is divine eros with the added richness of the sexual dimension.

But not all sexual relationships are true love relationships. It is possible to be in a sexual relationship without wishing for the other to be happy and fulfilled. If you don't truly love the other person in a sexual interaction, you are not too concerned about his or her happiness. In the absence of real love—when love is limited because of self-centeredness—the erotic interaction is bound to be limited as well. Yes, there is interaction and sexuality, and there can be sexual satisfaction and pleasure, but these are limited because the contact is self-centered; you are treating the other person mostly as an object for your satisfaction. This is not divine eros.

In contrast, if you truly love the other person, you are also seeing him or her as a subject, a center of consciousness. You love that center of consciousness and you want that consciousness to experience pleasure, to experience happiness, to experience delight. You feel very happy when you experience your partner being delighted.

When the sexually erotic interaction expresses selfless love in this way, you don't have an orgasm only when you have orgasm, you have an orgasm when your partner has one. You might not be having an orgasm, but when your beloved is, you are happier than she is. "Oh, beautiful!" You are happy that she is having such a good time. You can't do that if you don't really love her. If you don't love your partner, you are most likely thinking, "What about me? I'm not finished yet, not complete . . . maybe tomorrow . . ." And for some of us, "Maybe next month . . ."

Awakening Eros

We are exploring how to bring the erotic, including the sexual, into the context of reality and truth. We are discussing an enlightened kind of eroticism whose ground of mutual love awakens mutual desire. The mutual desire is to give each other pleasure, and by doing that, you both may experience the same pleasure—a pleasure that does not belong to either person. And because of the intense looping that is possible in these moments, the pleasure has no end. It grows deeper and more intense, and after a while, you don't know which one of you is having the good time. Actually, beyond a certain point, it doesn't matter who is having the good time, because the true divine erotic happens when you don't know.

It is not easy, and hence it is rare, to experience true love, the love that can say, "I enjoy your happiness, I want you to feel good and satisfied, and I will do whatever I can to make you happy. It makes me happy to give you joy and delight. I see that you are wonderful, and I want to give you whatever I can that recognizes your wonderfulness." We've also seen that we have difficulty experiencing desire. These days, many people don't even feel desire. They think, "Desire? What are you talking about? I've been liberated from desire a long time ago. I don't even know what it is." It is more common nowadays for a husband to ask his wife, "It would be nice to have a date . . . what do you think? Should we make it romantic tonight?" And the wife says, "Let's negotiate that. I think I might be up for it."

With divine eros, when desire happens sexually it's more like, "You are really sexy! God, you're beautiful . . . I didn't know I could feel this way about you." And she says, "But this is the kitchen!" And he answers, "Who cares? I don't want to wait until we go to the bedroom." You are not going to schedule yourself in for Tuesday night to make love. It's right now, baby, right now . . . You feel a dynamic force, a force you can't stop. And it's even better when the other person feels the same excitement: "Don't stop, baby, let's go; right now is perfect! Chair or table?" Actually, when the interaction is totally dynamic and spontaneous, you don't even ask, "Chair or table?"— both of you simultaneously choose the same place. It happens without communication. You just jump on it and it works because you feel each other.

If you really love one another, you have that openness and are interested in knowing the other, so communication is immediate. It just happens. This is a simpatico kind of love. We are not saying that sexually erotic love can't be soft, gentle, romantic, intimate, and sweet; we don't mean that it can't include tender kissing, whispering in his ear, nibbling on her neck. In fact, all these things are important expressions of erotic love. But divine eros expands the interaction in this sphere to the entire range of experience—from delicate, tender, and open to voluptuous, strong, and intense—all the way to powerful currents of passionate desire, powerful currents of erotic movement. After a while, you don't even know whether it is desire, love, or a rushing river of energy. They are all the same thing. True erotic interaction goes back and forth between all of these. It also is open to both sides—the active and the receptive, giving and taking.

You might not be involved in a sexually erotic relationship right now or you might feel the time for that has passed. We are presenting possibilities of what can happen between people when the right situation is present—and you never know when the right situation will be present! We are showing the potential of the erotic in human interactions when it is an expression of selfless love, so that we can learn how to extend our usual erotic relationships, whether sexual or not, into the spiritual sphere. Many of us are in such relationships now and are still young and healthy enough to engage their full potential. If we are not, it is good to know the potential of love relationships, for there might be more that is possible in our lives than we think.

Part of the difficulty of erotic relationships, especially the sexual ones, is that they can get into a rut. Habitual patterns become established: who is the pursuer and who is the pursued; who is active and who is passive; which one is the giver and which is the receiver; who initiates and who follows. When eroticism is free, when it is divine, it is not fixed; it is always in flux. Sometimes one of you is the active party, pursuing and initiating, and the next day it is the other person. And this can change even in the same interaction. Most people tend to stay in one role, and the other person takes on the opposite role. That is fine and can work for a while, but if it continues that way for too long, desire begins to die away. For erotic love to remain alive and renew itself, a mutual openness that opens the field is needed so that neither person assumes a particular role all the time. Who the active partner is and who is passive; which of you is powerful while the other is vulnerable; who is sweet and who is passionate . . . these roles can shift from one person to the other or you could both be the same way at the same time, at least occasionally.

One characteristic of divine eros that makes it a more complete expression of yourself is that you lose control. In a sexual encounter, there is a sense of surrender, of release, throughout the whole interaction, not only during orgasm. The absence of control, the release and surrender, is present all the way from the beginning. You lose control over your love, you lose control over your desire, and you lose control over your enjoyment, which makes the love, desire, and enjoyment arise more spontaneously and makes you less self-conscious and more at ease with each other.

As you might have already surmised, divine eros doesn't usually happen during one-night stands. A one-night stand can be passionate, can be intense, but it would be difficult for it to include love, mutuality, or the necessary sensitivity and attunement. The type of sensitivity in our emotional interactions that we have explored here needs to become much more expanded when physical interaction occurs. Because the physical dimension has its own sensitivity, it needs its own particular attunement. Part of that sensitivity is knowing where the other person is, which includes being aware of what hurts your partner and what gives her pleasure. You need the sensitivity and maturation that tells you what is too much and what is too little for her. And you need the capacity to respond in a way that optimizes the interaction so that it will deepen, intensify, and expand to reveal more of the potentials of that relationship.

ADDING THRILL TO OUR DISCOVERY

For the range of erotic interaction to expand, for the love to be passionate, and for the desire to be powerful, we need a quality of our true nature that is related to energy, to fire, to heat. We have already discussed qualities of our true nature such as personalness, kindness, sweetness, and empathy, and to complete the picture we now need to invite the presence of a fiery energy, a compact kind of excitement. It is a quality that gives a thrill to both love and desire, an excitement that courses through your blood such that you feel an intense bubbling from inside, both excited and full of pleasure at the same time. It is a state of excitation in which the presence of consciousness itself becomes a pure, thrilling excitement. It is like your blood beginning to feel hot in a thrilling, pleasurable way. You feel your body as if it were expanding into a luscious, delicious, fluid excitement.

Usually, we think of excitement as similar to electric energy, but think here of electricity that has been liquefied so that it is more palpable, more substantial. The substantiality is a more condensed excitement. It is the presence of aliveness. It is life in its purest quality. Our consciousness attains a vigorous quality, as a pure sense of excitation, of aliveness. This pure sense of vital presence can infuse the love, can infuse the desire, and we can then feel that our Being is ablaze. We become a big flame, a fluid flame, a flame of liquid, a liquid that is so excited that it combusts into consciousness ablaze. It shines and radiates but the heat is comfortable; it feels wonderful. You feel that you are alive with an excitement that doesn't agitate you; instead, it makes you feel good and happy.

This type of strong energy, this intensity of aliveness, this fiery quality, is a quality of our Being that needs to be liberated so that we can experience a desire that is powerful, uncontrollable, and that expresses life instead of expressing need. That is when the divine and the instinctual become one. This quality makes it possible for the divine—which is selfless, which is pure—and the instinctual—which is animal, powerful, and more sensuous—to combine and become completely inseparable. You can no longer distinguish between "Do I love?" and "Do I want?" They are the same thing. "Do I want to give pleasure or do I want to receive pleasure?" The mind can't even think about it. That is divine eros.

When we have this capacity, this strength of our Being, this expansive force of our Being, we can be strong in our desire, but this strength allows us to also be very delicate, very subtle, very refined, very gentle. Our gentleness doesn't come from weakness or passivity but from strength, from sufficiency. Depending on the situation, there can be an excitement in the intensity, or the same intensity can express itself as an exquisite, quite subtle appreciation, or as a delicate love, or a gentle enjoyment. It can also appear as a sense of movement toward one another so fine and deep that it is unstoppable. Or as a stillness in which the hearts of the two people come together as one.

We are getting closer to understanding divine eros . . .

We can see now that divine eros is not one monolithic thing: There isn't only one kind of intensity, and eros doesn't operate only on one level. Variety, change, and playfulness are all part of it. And when the playfulness is an expression of curiosity and discovery, even the sexually erotic situation becomes an inquiry, an arena of discovering reality. "Oh, I didn't know your neck feels this way. Let me see . . . let me lick it. Umm . . . yes . . . very different from your back." It is so intimate. And the other person says, "I like it when you touch me like that. Will you touch me more?" The next day, you find yourself interested in her knee. "Beautiful knee . . . look at the shape. How do you get it to look like that?" You are discovering new things—you are discovering your lover.

This is not a one-time event, it is a continual discovery. Your beloved is always new for you because you are always discovering new things about him. And, as you discover his body, you discover his soul, because his body is an entrance into his soul. As you discover his soul, you discover his spirit, and as you discover his spirit, you discover the spirit of the world. And as you discover the spirit of the world, you realize, "That's me! Here I am!" You entered through your heart and you came out as the nature of the universe. That is what we call a wormhole, a hole in the time-space continuum that transports us from one dimension to another without passing through time or space.

The power of the divinely sexual erotic situation is that it gives two people greater freedom to express themselves and to explore reality. With friends, you have a certain kind of freedom, relaxation, and ease because your sexuality is not involved—it's a whole charged area that you don't have to deal with. In explorations with a friend, you can tell them everything about you and they can tell you everything about them. This type of openness is not so easy in an erotic relationship that is sexual, because the physical contact brings into play hidden areas of heightened sensitivity related to our character and history. The emotional terrain tends to be more complex. However, if you can have that friendly openness and freedom in an erotic relationship that becomes physical, sensuous, and sexual, then the emotional and the physical dimensions are brought together, and there is no limit to what you can explore and how you explore it. You can do anything and say anything. With your friend, you can't do everything, but with a lover—if you both have the openness and mutual interest—there is no limitation to where and how you touch that person.

This adds a new dimension of exploration and discovery to the inquiry. The erotic interaction becomes a playful, enjoyable adventure of discovery. You are having pleasure, but through that pleasure you are discovering who you are and you are discovering reality. So you are experiencing not only physical pleasure but also the pleasure of discovery. The ordinary sexually erotic is only pleasure. The divine erotic is pleasure combined with discovering God—while you are experiencing the bliss of interaction, you are finding the divine in you and in the other, and in reality as a whole.

EROS AND SEX

I am making a distinction between the erotic and the sexual that will be very useful for many of us. Most of the time, when people use the word "erotic," they mean "sexual." But here we are using the word "erotic" to mean a heartfelt erotic in which there is love, there is sensuousness, there is enjoyment, there is desire and a desire for what is being enjoyed. The desire for enjoyment might mean a desire for intimacy, for contact, for communication, but since these ways of relating can be pleasurable and enjoyable without being sexual, they can happen even between friends. When erotic energy is present, you feel turned on, you feel alive; you really like the person and you like interacting with them. For example, you hear two friends talking about a subject they share a passion for. It feels as though they are making love, but they are actually talking about mathematics or a movie! I call that interaction "erotic" because it has a particular kind of aliveness, a pleasurable sense of a turn-on, but it doesn't necessarily include or lead to a desire for sexual, physical consummation.

When the erotic is sexual, it becomes more physical, it becomes more genitally oriented; you are interested in consummating in a physical interpenetration. The erotic involves interpenetration but not necessarily physical interpenetration; it is primarily on the soul level. "Erotic" means that the soul interaction—the communication, the looping and feedback—is very pleasurable, lively, and enjoyable. That is not the same thing as sexual interaction. "Sexual" means that the erotic interaction is focused on the physical dimension, and maybe the genital, which will make the relationship explicitly sexual. This means the erotic can move into a sexual expression if it is appropriate. If two people have the type of relationship where that can happen and agree that they both want it, then their connection can become sexual.

I am making this distinction because many of our spiritual experiences are erotic but not sexual. If you read the works of Christian mysticism, especially by some female saints, you will see that some are written in highly erotic language. The Song of Songs in the Old Testament is a good example; some of the Sufi poetry of Ibn 'Arabi and Rumi are others. The way these individuals talk about their experience with God is very sensual, voluptuous, full of desire and excitement, full of turn-on, but it is not physical and it is not sexual. This is true also in Indian mysticism. Many spiritual traditions have an erotic quality that embraces energy, desire, dynamism, pleasure, and blissfulness, but they are not exactly sexual.

Discriminating the erotic from the sexual allows us to integrate a new dimension of our spirituality. When you are meditating, for instance, you can have a meditation experience with your true nature that has a very erotic quality. You feel as though you were making love with reality, but it is not really sexual, although sometimes it has many of those same pleasurable and exciting qualities that you can even experience at the same level of intensity. The more the erotic energy is liberated, the more it is free to infuse any area of life with sensual, vibrant, pleasurable presence. The erotic quality can manifest sometimes between good friends and frequently occurs in the dialectic inquiry practice that we do. Eros can lead to further spiritual liberation if we use the energy to open the dialectic field and find new ways of expression beyond the physical.

EXPLORATION SESSION

We will do an exercise now to practice finding some new ways to express eros and to open up the field to divine eros. You will be making three inquiries, spending ten to fifteen minutes on each. This can be done either with another person or as a writing exercise on your own. If you are with a partner, take turns exploring the first question, then the second, then third. When it is your turn to listen, be a silent witness, not interrupting or giving feedback but attuning to your partner in a neutral, caring way.

1. Explore what limits your experience of the erotic. We all have experiences of feeling erotic or being erotic; here you want to explore what limits these experiences. Also, you might experience the erotic in certain ways but not in others. Why? What is in the way of the expansion of eros in your life? What prevents it from having a bigger range, more intensity, more depth, more subtlety? We have opened up the meaning of erotic to include more qualities and more variety to give you the opportunity to see what else is possible for you.

2. Explore what makes you keep your erotic desires separate from your heart. You can be erotic without eros being divine, without it including selfless, giving love. This is quite normal. But we have been studying the divine erotic, where love and desire mix and

become one, which means that our heart and our genitals are not separate. Love usually flows through the heart, and erotic desire flows through the pelvic center, whether the desire is erotic or simply sexual. In divine eros, you cannot have erotic energy or sexual contact without love. Love brings your aliveness, your erotic feelings, into the heart, which is the seat of interaction. This erotic completeness requires an openness between these two centers, a complete exchange between the pelvis and the heart. There is no barrier because love and desire combined means that the pelvis and the heart are not disconnected. Many of us can feel love, or we can feel erotic desire, but having them both arise in one experience will bring up the limitations in our erotic maturation. You want to see what makes you want to keep your pelvis and your heart separate.

Be spontaneous in this exploration; don't try to be reasonable, because you want to see your unconscious reasons for keeping the two apart. You might feel, for example: "Even the idea scares the hell out of me" or "I would need my lover forever." "I'd never be able to work; I'd have to have sex all the time." "Love reminds me of loving my mother, and eros is something different. If I bring them together, it's a no-no . . . it's dangerous . . . it's too much." You might find yourself saying to a lover, "If my heart and my genitals were totally connected, I would never want to be away from you." Whatever it is, let it come out. We have many reasons for keeping the two separate. Some of us have difficulty with love, some of us have difficulty with desire. Most of us have difficulty bringing them together, making them one.

3. Explore the ways you actually experience the unity of love and sexuality. This is explicitly about sexuality, not simply being erotic, so you want to look at the experience of love and sexuality together. How do you experience that? What is it like for you? You might feel, "What are you talking about? They are not united." Or "It's out of this world." Or you might just want to say, "Yum, yum, yum!"

QUESTIONS AND COMMENTS

Student: I did the exercise with somebody I didn't know before and it was a man. I thought, "These are very difficult questions to explore with somebody I don't know, and who is of the other sex." What I am feeling now is boundlessness. What I experienced didn't have to do so much with him. It had to do only with myself. The feeling is that there are no boundaries.

Hameed: You were exploring yourself, so it makes sense that it has to do with yourself. When you feel there are no boundaries, what is that like? What does that mean? Does it mean you don't have a size?

Student: Yes, it is unusual. I am shaky, but it is open and it's light.

Hameed: Boundaries make things close down, although we believe we need them. We feel shaky without them because we feel that we are not held together, we're not protected. But it feels open and light. So if you feel the openness and the lightness itself, if you stay with that, what happens? Does it get more or less or something else?

Student: There comes also a different joy, a different power.

Hameed: Where do you feel it?

Student: It comes out of the belly. And it goes up here into my chest.

Hameed: You are smiling. You like that different power? As you feel this good power, tell me more about it. What kind of sensation is it?

Student: It is something strong, but it is light. It has strength. And it doesn't go away. It stays there.

Hameed: As it comes up, does it fill you more?

Student: Big. I feel big.

Hameed: That's one thing that happens when we lose our boundaries—we lose our sense of size. We don't have the same size. We're expanded. That is one meaning of "expanded"—an expansive state that has that energy, that nice sense of power. What happened to the shakiness?

Student: It is still there, but it doesn't matter. It's not important.

Hameed: Sounds like you are more important.

Student: Yes.

Hameed: That's great.

Student: Thank you.

Student: The continuum in my childhood was my love for God and the love of the unnameable. That was the continuum where I felt I could give my love. The question we explored was like torturing the humanness in me. It felt like betrayal of God. It felt that touching the sexual part was like touching the soul and the child with this immense pure love and dedication for the unnameable. I was often in the church and praying. I had my conversations with the unnameable.

Hameed: I like "the unnameable." "Unnameable" sounds like a good way of saying it.

Student: I saw in the inquiry that I got loved by the unnameable. It was a mutual love there that brought me through, but at the same time, it was in some way dissociating from being a human in this life.

I felt like I could burst in tears in despair when inquiring into this area. At the end of the inquiry, I felt an enormous energy in me that was opening me. My heart was beating very strongly, and it was like my physical body was filled up with energy. It was like a breakthrough of what I had excluded. And my love for the unnameable has even more strength. But now the physical is included.

All of me is just loving this. It feels like a small opening, but it is so strong in me that I feel that when it is more digested, it could also be in a relationship with a human being.

Hameed: Your connection to the divine can include the physical. Your body is part of you, and that presence can fill the body; it comes through it. You saw that the body becomes transparent to it.

Student: It seems so important to me that it is okay that the body is here or that my cells open up to the divine, even the divine in a human being.

Hameed: It is important that it comes through the body.

Student: Yeah, that the body is holy or divine because it is filled with this substance that is holy.

Hameed: That is beautiful. It seems you are happy with that. You are having a direct experience of what we mean by "divine eros." It is love in interaction with the erotic dimension. It is divine, it is holy. And we can experience this holiness as our connection with the divine. But the same holiness, the same energy, can happen in an interaction with another human being. The body can be sacred that way . . . and that is the way into the sacred; it is a way that the erotic becomes divine. It can also be the way into sacred sexuality.

Student: In the sense of unification, in the sense of celebration of unification, and the celebration of humanness of us as human beings.

Hameed: You got it—the celebration of unification.

———————————

Student: I saw how speaking the truth in relationship is somehow very exciting and sometimes very sexual. Being honest about what I experience ignites the sexuality.

Hameed: Being honest, and feeling that we have erotic energy, doesn't mean we have to have sex. It can mean that, but not necessarily.

Student: I am not saying exactly that I feel erotic; I am just being honest about whatever is happening inside. The humanness is important in that moment to communicate.

Hameed: How do you feel now?

Student: It feels freeing that this is true. It is also childlike. In a way, the fear that I exist—to be honest about it—makes it exciting.

Hameed: The fear can turn into excitement when we are courageous. There might be fear, but if we don't retreat because of the fear, then it can become exciting, it can come alive.

Student: Seeing the barriers to the unity of heart and pelvis opened up things in a big way. I felt that everything was available—strength, courage, fire, and energy. That became a huge resource in the third inquiry, including the sensitivity, and that was quite an amazing experience. I started to look at the other as an object but not only as that. There was something precious, almost divine, in my partner.

Hameed: That is exactly what happens when we include love with our sexuality: The other is not just an object anymore. The other is partly an object but they are also a soul. That is beautiful to see. That is really what love can make happen.

Music Meditation

Suggested Selections:

"Niobe's Theme" and "Cleopatra Seduces Caesar," from the album *Rome: Music from the HBO Series* (soundtrack CD by Jeff Beal)

The two selections are to be played sequentially. This music meditation will involve a visualization. As you listen to the music, allow yourself to see and feel a deliciously warm, liquid fire coming into your feet. It is fire in the sense that it feels red, glowing, and shiny—but it is liquid, full and warm. It doesn't burn you. It feels like a delicious warmth. It comes into the feet and slowly fills your legs . . . fills the pelvis . . . and then moves to fill your whole body. This warmth has a particular sensation, a particular kind of pleasure. It is not just fire—it is thrill and pleasure and the aliveness of our energy, of our essential nature.

This combination of thrill, pleasure, and aliveness—this thrilling aliveness—is like what you feel right before orgasm. You are enjoying very beautiful lovemaking, and just before your orgasm, there is a particular feeling. It is not the orgasm itself, it is just before the orgasm, when you feel this beautiful, expanding delicious pleasure that wants to complete itself. It is pleasure that is dynamic, that is naturally moving toward completion, toward becoming more of itself. It is a thrilling kind of pleasure that you don't have control over, and it is arising from the bottom of your feet as liquid pleasure, with a red, fiery color, arising and filling you until it fills you all up.

Your body might not even have a shape as it opens and expands. That is one way of experiencing who we are, our nature. So you visualize this thrilling, orgasmic kind of aliveness, filling you up as you listen to the music. And the music helps you get the feel, get the flavor.

8

———

Desire for Union

KAREN

WE ARE GOING TO START this session a little bit differently today. I would like everybody to stand up. We will do the OM salutation in a particular way, followed by a music meditation. Then we will finish with the Kath meditation.

Our body is the vehicle through which we express ourselves in the world. When we are communicating, when we are going through our daily life, our body is the vehicle of expression through walking, talking, thinking, and so on. So we want to give our body its due and let it respond to the energies that are arising.

In the OM salutation, you are going to bring in the three centers—the head, the heart, and the belly—appreciating each one for its unique function in life. As you make the OM sound, each center is brought into consciousness as you move your hands from above the head past that center. Each center expresses, respectively, a particular function on the inner journey: the desire and capacity to know (head), your love of the truth (heart), and your embodiment of your nature and its action in the world (belly).

For the head center, your palms are together at the top of the forehead with the fingers pointing up. For the heart center, bring your hands down together, so that your fingers point outward from the heart at the center of chest. For the belly, your hands move to the belly center, fingers pointing downward toward the ground. Once you have completed the OM salutation, you wait silently for the music to begin and then as you listen, let it move you.

MUSIC MEDITATION

Suggested Selection:

"Cleopatra Seduces Caesar," from the album *Rome: Music from the HBO Series* (soundtrack CD by Jeff Beal)

This music is sensuous and sexy, with a deep bass tone and a sinuous rhythm. Listening to the music, your eyes can be open or closed. You can move your body with the energy or just let the energy move through you. Be where you are and let it impact you. At the end of the piece, stand for a few minutes. Then you may either sit down or remain standing to do the Kath meditation. If you prefer to stand, hold your hands in the same position as when you sit, with hands clasped, right hand holding the left and the left hand clasping the right thumb. Maintain your presence at the belly center and continue to let the energy flow.

THE OPEN-HEARTED FIELD

I always find it a little bit difficult to talk after dancing to this music because the energy is so overwhelming, so overpowering and delicious, that it speaks for itself. But I'll give it a go. I thought it was odd that so many electronic devices were going off and making sounds (many cell phones rang during the meditation). Then I began to feel that each one of us was an electronic device—and in some sense, that is actually true. As individuals, we are conduits for a very special kind of electricity that ignites us and illuminates the world with its spark. Actually, the work we are doing here is all about becoming a divine lightbulb, a luminous globe of light.

When we start our life in the world, that light is still burning bright. When we see the birth of an infant, we are amazed, touched, and moved by the power and miracle of a being coming into the world. It is one of those experiences in life that have a deep impact on us. Another one is watching life leaving the world, seeing the process of the living light of the soul transitioning to another realm. The power of the experiences of birth and death is awesome and humbling.

Part of what makes it so is the sense of the completely unknown miracle of it, the amazing dominance of nature taking over and asserting her spirit, rendering us totally out of control. At these moments, we recognize that we are at the effect of the life force, and that it is far more immense than we are. The moments of birth and death are among the few times when the average individual comes into contact with the magnificent energy, momentum, and thrust of this force, which manifests life and absorbs it back into itself.

If any of you have ever been in the room when a woman is giving birth, you can't help but be in touch with a sense of awe at the immensity of this energetic explosion. The same is true for witnessing death and the power of the silence that dominates in those moments. We have to be very coarse, very thickened, to not feel that in some way.

Of course, people go through all kinds of difficult times in childbirth, but in the end, when we see that little foot or little head (depending on which way the baby arrives), we seem to get that a living being is coming into the world as a body. We gasp and take note of the miracle. The room illuminates with energy and life. The heart opens, tears flow. Feelings flood in, in ways that we never could have imagined. Love is ignited, and everybody in the room seems to be engulfed in a field of energetic aliveness and powerful love.

The opportunity to be in such a field exists not only at the beginning or end of life, but also within the relationships we have throughout our lives. Enlivening these relationships means liberating the energy of creation within the shared field. We can create a birth canal through our friendships and love relationships. We touch one another's hearts and souls if we are open to that . . . but openness is not enough. We can't just sit and wait for the miracle; we also need to apply ourselves and orient our attention in such a way that we invite presence into the process. Communicating well, sharing experiences, or even having good sex is not what enables our relationships to deepen. Many people experience some of these things in relationship, and that is a good thing, but there can be much more, as we have been discussing.

Everybody has some sexual energy—some people more than others. Engagement in sexual pleasure is part of a normal and natural encounter for those who are in a couple relationship. Some of you may have chosen not to be sexual or aren't in a relationship, so you feel erotic energy only with the inner beloved. Erotic energy exists within us as life energy and is simply a part of what and who we are, regardless of the ways it may or may not be expressed. And divine eros is a potential of that energy that is heartful, alive, and sensual.

Erotic energy can become a force that animates our spiritual experiences and spiritual lives. We can live in the world with eros as part of the being that we are when our erotic energy is freely manifesting in many areas of our experience. In effusive ways, expansive ways—but also in small and in the most delicate of ways—our life energy can express and fortify our developing consciousness in any of its qualities and dimensions. Just being who we are, whether we are in a very intimate relationship with one person or intimately involved in our friendships, we have companions on the path, on the journey with us.

The beautiful thing about human beings is that we can face each other and have the kind of connection that echoes the connection with our inner nature. We are a species that can consciously know ourselves and engage in relationship as two sides of the same thing in a way that allows our inner world, our inner universe, to touch and to blend with another universe. The possibility of two consciousnesses creating an inimitable configuration while remaining authentically themselves is part of an intelligent creative potential for us. To be two as one field, grounded in the deep vastness of eternity, is a special and wonderful possibility.

THE DRIVE THAT OPENS US

The sex drive begins as the drive for procreation. We were first conscious of this as the drive to create a charged connection based on attraction. If you can, remember when you were thirteen. Many of us experienced the out-of-control feeling of hormonal surges while sitting in class and checking out the girls or the guys. It might have been, "Forget studying; let's pass notes!" or perhaps, "Even the teacher is looking very yummy—better watch out!" Before you know it, you're saying to yourself, "Oh my God, this is out of control. No, I can't do this." Then the cute one in the next row gets your attention, and you push the feelings away, trying to control yourself: "No, I have to concentrate on math." When you're that age, everybody starts to look like an erotic object. And if you can't find anybody, you go home, shut the door, and take care of yourself.

Sexual energy arises naturally at that time in our lives; it is pulsing and flowing at full strength. Growing up, we learn to be more appropriate with our energy. As we mature, the hormones calm down a bit, and we are also better able to sublimate that creative urge. We take pleasure in our creative pursuits, our desire for knowledge, the expression of our skills and talents, and so on. Sexual excitement becomes relegated to certain times and certain places.

If you sense into your body right now, can you remember that glorious feeling of being overrun by this powerful energy? Maturity does not have to mean that we no longer have access to this part of ourselves. We are different now than when we were thirteen, of course; we're not run by our hormones anymore. In fact, some of us are starting to feel, "Where did all those hormones go? I don't care anymore about being overrun by them. I just want the regular stuff they do!"

Testosterone and estrogen are servants of this energy, not the other way around. They are the transmitters of the life force and its erotic quality. They are the biological channeling of energy but don't entirely determine its functioning. We all know that our emotional life has a great impact on our energetic potential, for instance. The more liberated the energy, the more we can continue to feel and enjoy our erotic life, and the less limited it will be by our biology and moods.

Although the sexual drive begins as the urge to procreate, it is also mixed with the urge for pleasure. As a species, we have continual access to sexual energy and to sexual enjoyment, and we don't necessarily have to procreate. Birth control has been a major advancement in this area. We can have sex and pleasure without bringing a child into the world unless we want to. It is possible to choose how we use our sexual energy so that it is expressed at the right time, in the right places, with the right people.

We can go even further now and explore how we can mature to the point where we can allow our divinity to come through with that energy, which means that the presence of both our sexual energy and our love can be united as one force. This opens up a new realm that enables us to mature further, and in new ways.

Thus the drive for pleasure can become the energy that opens us up to a new arena in our development. As we discussed earlier, to fully know ourselves as mature beings means that we become individuals who are able to fully be and express our true nature in a pure and simple way. We learned that the pleasure we seek comes from our nature and that we do not have to find it in the physical realm, although we can. We can know pleasure as distinct from the drive for pleasure or from the drive to procreate, and in this way feel the pleasure of being. We are a being of presence with the ability to know ourselves completely in the now, without being defined by our own or someone else's ideas of who we are. This is deeply blissful.

When we are in touch with the depth of our essential heart, we are able to be filled with the presence of sweet nectars. It is possible for us to not only feel the effect of these nectars, as in the usual experience of emotional love, but also to feel the heart in its natural condition as the presence of a loving, fluid richness. The heart that has reconnected with its depth is a fountain of bliss.

The Desire for Union

Desire can lead us to the distillation of itself, as an energy that we reconnect to. Desire in the human being can be felt as instinctual or emotional. Instinctually, it can arise as the sexual drive or as a drive toward self-preservation of the physical body. But the pure energy that is the origin of this force can blend with the purity of essential love, so that we can rise to another level of experience that combines the love of the heart and the drive of the life force. The driven power of the energy that was once focused on procreation combines with the love that melts boundaries between our own soul and the Beloved to become one powerful force that culminates in a drive for union.

This is the type of feeling we have for or with another person when we are in love. It can arise in a way that is fortified by union with our true nature, in which both of us are deeply in touch with the infinite nature of Being and are bursting into existence together with the power of life. We are born afresh and new—full, rounded, beautiful beings of divine nature within the field of the relationship. We are united with the depth of Being, the depth of our nature, and with each other, all as one unity. The Beloved that lives in our heart is the core of this type of relating. In this unity, we know that we are that and can never be separated from it or from each other.

Eternal presence permeates everything all of the time, whether we are conscious of it or not. Many things are possible because of this truth. When we feel ourselves in touch with this presence, we can feel the power of it arising as energy. We feel it bubbling up like a fountain, an upwelling in the fullness of love. Then it is possible to feel a desire that no longer is a longing for what we are missing. Instead, we want to share and connect with another of like kind who is from our home, from the deep and awesome nature that is our source. Our humanity shows itself as the wave that is full of its ocean, wanting to share itself with another of the same ocean.

The physical body is one way that our individual consciousness appears in the world. Each body and form is unique and beautiful as the expression of the one consciousness appearing as many. The ocean of consciousness can express itself as currents of uniqueness that can feel the pull toward one another with a fullness, velocity, intensity, and energy. Rather than a hunger spawned by a sense of missing something, it is a wanting to give and a wanting to receive at the same time. The desire to unite is the expression of the ocean that knows itself as the unity arising as currents within it and that feels a charge, an attraction between those currents. The currents—particular individuals, each a unique consciousness expressing the ocean of our nature—sense this energy and desire between them since they are fundamentally not separate from one another.

It starts as a connection or an attraction. As the attraction grows, the connection increases and you feel the love that is connecting the two of you. The love opens up the desire to engage in sharing your experiences. You all know that this feels inherently good and fulfills you in some way. But you also have the potential to develop this capacity with a deeper ground and meaning. It is a pleasure, a joy and delight, to be able to look into each other's eyes, feel into each other's hearts, and touch one another physically as one united presence expressing itself as two.

We can feel this desire for union, and the experience of union as connection, in various degrees and in any form of relationship—in friendships, with our children or parents, with a lover. There are many kinds of relationships, but I'm thinking of two kinds in particular at the moment. There is the type of friendship where we are companions on the journey—we connect, we help each other support the truth in one another, with a mutual sense of having the other's best interests at heart. A real friend challenges you where you can't see yourself and loves you in the process. He or she can accept you as you are and at the same time encourage you to keep growing and expanding. And you give each other encouragement to take the risks needed, becoming more vulnerable to one another and more transparent to your limitless nature. A real friendship has at its roots the willingness to see the truth. And that's a gift you both give to the world.

Sexual lovers are all of the former, or can be, with the added component of the erotic expressing itself in physical ways. The sexual lover is one with whom the physical is a conduit for the drive for union to express itself in a more complete way.

Whether or not sexual expression is part of a relationship, the desire for union expresses itself in the desire to rend the veils between you and the other. Erotic energy expresses itself in helping each other become more naked by exposing and enjoying the beauty and the awe of the energetic union. This naturally invites more of it to manifest. There's a palpable feeling of connection as you both become more in touch with the presence and the sweetness of connection. This gives rise to the joy and the celebration of connection as you go deeper into the discovery of your partner and the shared field as one movement.

Moving through delights and difficulties together is part of the sharing and the discovery of more ways that the relationship can manifest its infinite possibilities. We feel losses and disappointments, and these are all opportunities to be born again into another level of relationship. It is scary, hard, and painful—and it's beautifully sublime. Nobody ever said it was easy.

Divine eros sounds so good. It *is* goodness. It is pure goodness. It is the presence of purity, of energy, of an awesome pleasure beyond anything you can ever imagine. It's a powerful motivation and drive for being yourself and being willing to feel the truth of whatever you're feeling, regardless of circumstances. Divine eros is a way you can experience your inner nature. How much do you want that for yourself? For another? We have the opportunity to enjoy the connection on the various levels of relating, but some of us find that our lover is in our friend because he or she loves the same thing that we love, and that is what we share. And when we share the love for the depth of truth, it creates the foundation that the relationship connection needs in order to continue to spiral to ever greater depths.

In the case of sexual lovers, the desire to unite can reach a level of intensity of wanting to embrace each other simply to feel the union of the shared field. You want the union to be as complete as possible. The beauty of the physical dimension is that souls can interpenetrate on a new level, the physical, but it is not 100 percent interpenetration since human bodies remain distinct. The desire of the essential heart for complete union can lead to the discovery that something exists that can transcend the physical while including it, unifying the hearts, bodies, and minds of both people as one. The yearning to be inside one another arises with uncontrollable energy and love. The desire, the wanting to unite in every way possible, completely and totally, continues to expand and deepen, into territory where eros can manifest and create new forms of experience.

DIVINE UNION

Our nature, which is the depth of reality, is oneness, a complete unity, and it is deep, silent, and still. But this absolute nature of ours does not live alone. It is always in divine union with its consort—the creative power and energy that brings everything forward into manifestation. There is the unmanifest and there is the manifest, which are two sides of the same thing. It is not that manifestation comes out of the unmanifest, which is behind it. Yes, there is the unmanifest back and the manifest front, and if you slice them, there is yet again a back and a front at every point; but the spaciousness of the unmanifest and the presence of the manifest always arise as one interpenetrated unity. Within physical manifestation we have both the depth of our nature and the surface of the particular forms, which are always in union, always as one.

A relationship between two people can reflect this reality when we feel the drive to be in union. Two individuals can actually express it completely, unified as one field of presence that contains both the receptive and the active as one energy flow. The more each of you is embodying all the attitudes that reflect the pure qualities of the natural condition of being open, receptive, active, and assertive, the more you will experience balance and energy in a creative rhythmic dance that is expressing the unity of the universe. So the erotic can be felt within any relationship that has the energy, love, and drive for the truth and discovery. It might not result in the interpenetration of bodies, but it can be the interpenetration of souls, which is very satisfying in itself.

Sometimes when we are exploring this kind of connection, we think we might lose ourselves. That is actually the beauty of it, not a problem. But we need to feel ourselves in our maturity as the presence of a true person—a presence that is a form of our nature that can be lost and arise again, spontaneously and naturally. We don't have to feel that we are a person all the time. We can be a delicate, sweet puddle or we can be a thriving, throbbing mass aflame with the passionate presence of our nature. Or we can be nothing, absolutely nothing at all. The more freedom we have, the more fluidly we can change form in our experience.

In fact, this characteristic of realization is something else that we have no control over. Our experience is changing all the time. We cannot keep it to one tone or quality. A personal form will manifest when it needs to, but if we are insecure in our personhood, in the sense of who we are, this will limit the forms we can take. It is good to know that there are other possibilities. I find for myself that when I hit a limit to how far I can let myself go, it is nothing but another opportunity. What do I think I'm going to lose if I give myself over? I'm only going to lose another idea of myself.

We hold those ideas of ourselves near and dear. It is difficult to let them go because we do not fully recognize that they are ideas. But when desire for union intensifies, they naturally get exposed as being ideas and it becomes natural to let go of them. However, this doesn't happen by an active process of getting rid of them; through exposing them, they are rendered transparent and become part of the fuel for the fire of love. The erotic energy in service of the spirit will drive you to keep confronting any barriers and burn away whatever stands between you and your beloved. Many of these barriers are the ideas that define our reality and limit what we are and can be.

THE PASSION TO REUNITE

On the spiritual journey, our drive to reunite is most fundamentally with our deepest nature. The drive usually starts out as a feeling of wanting intimacy with another human being, with God, or with the natural world. Our drive to seek that union begins with a very important orientation toward, and a potent interest and engagement in, the spiritual, but it builds into an out-of-control drive for union. We want something so desperately and so fully that we can't help but feel our heart bursting with love for it. We want it with everything we've got, and we give the gift of ourselves, for the self that is holding back is what's in the way.

One of the things we say when we are in the throes of passion—when we want our lover so much and feel such love for that person—is "Take me, take all of me—leave nothing behind! I want to give myself to you 100 percent!" There is a drive to give ourselves fully—no trying involved, just a natural giving. We want to take off that last cloak.

We can feel this toward God, our Beloved: "I don't want to feel separate from you anymore. I want you here. I want you here with me *now*. So come on! I want you, and I will give you everything." We don't even know exactly what that is. It is not an image in the mind. In fact, the more that the images of what we've been thinking we want fade away, the more we feel the wanting. The love and passion are for the mystery itself. The heart knows what it wants without the mind getting involved: "I don't even know what you look like, and I'm willing to do anything. I've never met you completely, but I want you."

You want to be completely united, and that is why you say, "Take me." You want to know what it's like to have nothing come between you. You've taken off your clothes, you've become more transparent, but you want to go even further, to dissolve every last thing that remains that keeps you from being able to feel total union with the divine. You feel that you are in the realm of the gods. You are a god or a goddess expressing the universe, and you are in divine embrace.

When you fall in love with someone, that person is the most beautiful human being you have ever seen. And in your eyes, it's an objective fact: He is the man of all men and the most handsome; she is the most beautiful, the woman that embodies the essence of all women. "I want to dive into those eyes . . . I want to be in him," you say to yourself, and he is thinking the same thing about you. You dive into each other and then you come up for air and look at one another—and then you do it again and again. You keep finding more ways to dive. You dive into his heart and into his body; he dives into you, back and front and sideways. You keep finding new places to dive into . . . and then there is just the simple reality of the blended consciousness that is not one and not two.

There is no difference between feeling this with another person and feeling it in relation to our nature. It is the same process, the same energy, the same eros. We feel the yearning and the desire that becomes the fuel for the process of unification. The energy of divine eros springs forth from the eternity and vastness of what we are, and the focus doesn't have to be only in one place or on one person. All of manifestation is created, instant by instant, by this force. When we tap into it and liberate it from the merely instinctual realm, we have the opportunity to be with another person in a way that expresses that force as the ecstasy of union. We become an external expression of an internal reality.

The erotic is divine. Divine eros is your birthright and it was present in its purity upon your entrance into this world. It was all there, coemergent—your naked body and the intense, bursting energetic life force of the divine. To awaken to this beauty and magnificence once again through the spiritual gate is one of the splendid blessings of this life.

EXPLORATION SESSION

This is a three-part exploration done with a partner.

1. Begin by taking turns exploring and inquiring into the ways you each experience the desire for union. Take ten to fifteen minutes each. As you do this, let your understanding come up spontaneously, in any way it is arising for you. You may not be feeling the desire for union, for example—talk about that and how it feels. Or you may notice that you feel some interest in this question or about something that has been said today. Whatever is there for you might arise in ways that you can't imagine or foresee. Find the thread of where you are and follow it in.

2. Engage in a dialectic inquiry with your partner, exploring the field between you. You each want to engage in exploring the relationship and the field that you are sharing together. Spend twenty to thirty minutes doing this.

3. Have a discussion with your partner: How did that quality of union arise? Did you feel connected? Did you feel that you were experiencing presence, togetherness, some kind of oneness? If you felt united, how did you experience that? Was it as two people who had a connection or did it go all the way to feeling that you were one?

Remember that there is no correct state that you are supposed to get to. This exploration is about where you are in relation to union. You want to invite the truth of your experience and be exactly where you are. That will enable the next step, whatever it is, to happen. Don't try to unite. Just be where you are and let it happen naturally.

QUESTIONS AND COMMENTS

Student: There was a very strong interaction between my partner and me, particularly in the heart area. During the dialectic, when the forces were combining between us, I felt there was a very strong power that could be used for the world. And then when we were discussing our interaction, my partner said that the intimacy was lacking. That part was more difficult.

There was also a strong effect from yesterday's session on sexual love that left me depressed. I think it is good to inquire into the sadness that got evoked about how this basic energy has been used in so many destructive ways. For me it is such a load, on a national scale as well as personally. For example, what they did to my mother, and feeling my solidarity with women . . . how sexuality was a matter of cutting away the genitals. Also how many scars are needed to hide the basic power—all the killing, the wars that happened in this land; it is quite a lot. All of that is in the way of being in touch in a more positive way with my basic power.

Karen: Are you saying you are feeling more in touch in a positive way with your basic power right now, or that you want to be?

Student: I was feeling many things that were still in the way, the load that has to be worked through or has to be made conscious; it is quite a pressure.

Karen: And that is something we find when we start to be in touch with this energy: It brings out more of the unconscious. There is a lot to this energy. It has both sexual and aggressive energies in it that we have used for survival purposes. The ways we have expressed it in the world or kept it repressed will come up more because we are exploring this. It is also important to recognize that being in touch with our nature is what is necessary before we start considering expressing it.

It is a double-edged sword. Becoming more present brings out issues that we need to work through. Eventually, we learn that we can express this energy in a positive way; we can learn to express it with sensitivity, tenderness, kindness, and consciousness, but also with power. What we realize is that the power of our erotic nature is not a destructive one. It always comes with love. The motivation for creation is love.

Surrendering to this energy is not a passive thing. It is a melting into our true nature, which imbues us with creative capacity in a real way. We can then be courageous and be vulnerable at the same time, because that is what it means to be who we are.

Student: For me, indeed the only solution is to have the connection with the heart, with love; otherwise, there's no way.

Karen: Exactly. There are many levels of being in touch and connected. And it can go very deep; we become more and more vulnerable to ourselves and to the other. But we don't need to take it further than we are able to at any given time. We take a step, let things arise, see what they are, and some of that unconscious load becomes visible to us. We can understand it more, feel the interaction, feel the vulnerability, and it starts all over again, so we get a little deeper and a little more light, transparent, each time.

I was shy, once upon a time. The power of this was frightening to me. I had to deal with a lot to be able to handle it. There is a power in the world that destroys and is hurtful. This is the ignorant action of distorted power . . . but what the power of being destroys are the veils that separate us: "I want to be near you and I don't want anything to be between us." So the more we trust, the more we can let that power come forward. Don't push it. Be kind. This basic goodness has gentleness and sensitivity, and patience. So we just do what we can. That's all.

Student: Thank you for saying you were shy. I've been shy. It made me ask for the mike. I am trembling all over. I had a beautiful experience, but . . . no "but"! It was a beautiful experience, but . . .

I said it again!

Karen: Somebody keeps saying that "but."

Student: Always.

Karen: Who is that?

Student: For now it is a little boy, and he is walking around with his hands up high, not knowing what to do . . . just wandering around, no ground beneath his feet.

Karen: Let yourself shake and feel your belly. Maybe you could ask your neighbor to hold the mike for you. Just shake and take a breath . . . Now, what are you feeling in your belly?

Student: There is warmth . . . there is warmth and I can feel a strong connection with the floor.

Karen: Feel the warmth . . . And how does that little boy feel when he feels the warmth—is he still there?

Student: Yeah. He doesn't understand a thing about what is happening.

Karen: When you feel the warmth, is it okay to not understand what is happening?

Student: No.

Karen: Is he scared because he doesn't understand?

Student: He's scared. He's a nice little boy as well.

Karen: I can tell. Sensitive, isn't he?

Student: Yes.

Karen: Take some deep breaths. How are you feeling? What are you afraid of?

Student: I want to tell you something. I know why that little boy is wandering around and doesn't know what to do. I think the ground around me was falling away yesterday, and it was okay. Not that it's nice, but this desire thing . . . all the time, for years, I've been working for a peaceful mind and I'm very grateful that now and then and often I can feel a peaceful mind. There was a time when desire was taking over; my desire and the desire for sexuality took me. Looking back, I could say that maybe it was an addiction . . . addicted to sex. And coming out of that brought me a lot of distance from desire, just taking a look at it and not going in. Now I feel there is also a power I felt there. Getting to feel that desire here, I am so afraid of becoming an addict again.

Karen: Let's hang out with the energy for a minute. Just feel the warmth in your belly and don't do anything about it. There is nothing to do. What do you feel when you feel the warmth?

Student: It's good. It's moving all over. It is still here.

Karen: Take some deep breaths. Let it go down your legs.

Student: That is the difficult part.

Karen: What is difficult about letting it go down your legs? What happens? What does it hit that stops it?

Student: I just don't trust it.

Karen: Feel your lack of trust. What don't you trust about it? You don't need to do anything to anybody or yourself here. Just feel the lack of trust and keep sensing the warmth as it expands. Let's see what it wants to do, not what you want to do with it.

Student: When the warmth goes down my legs, it's just like the world can have my weight, and it isn't that much.

Karen: It might be more than you think.

Student: Point taken.

Karen: Are you feeling like you're more on the floor? How does that feel?

Student: I like it and it feels a bit unknown now.

Karen: This energy is helping to ground you; it's not letting you fly off into your fantasy. A good practice for you is to stay with the Kath meditation, and also to sense your legs. Notice when they are not there . . . what happens, what's keeping the energy from moving down. Your fear was that you would act out; now you are just solid.

Student: I am here.

Karen: You are more here. Hello! And you don't look like a little boy. You look like a man. It seems that not letting the energy move down is what gets you into your history, your fantasies, your need to sexually act out. Maybe it was a distorted way to get the grounding, but you can use the energy to do that instead.

Student: Thank you.

Student: I made a discovery. I woke up very early and I felt my neck burn, my throat burn, and then I felt I could surrender. Images came about losses, and when we just did inquiry, I had this fantasy to ask for support or to share, and I didn't know how to do it. I felt what you were saying earlier . . . to just go for it. I felt my energy was there to do that, but I was so afraid that people wouldn't respond to me. That's it.

Karen: What's happening as you say it now? What happens when you go for it?

Student: My energy bursts out . . . or it's just there . . . but it is a step to really go for it and not fantasize about all the people and what their reactions are. It is a big step to be totally autonomous.

Karen: Yes, autonomy is a step into maturity. And it's the blend of how to be yourself and keep the connection. If we feel that the connection is necessary in order to be ourselves, we may sacrifice ourselves for the connection. But when we are being ourselves fully and completely, the connection becomes an expression of our love. You just spoke it beautifully.

There are many people here feeling something similar; so how do we have that balance? We get attached to the connection and give ourselves up or else we are autonomous, not needing the connection—but what about having both? When faced with a choice, take both. In fact, it is not a choice; we do need both because both of these are aspects of ourselves. We are individuals and we are part of one another.

Student: I am happy for that because it was already a desire, but I didn't let it come fully. I was concerned about people's reactions.

Karen: You didn't see the truth in the desire; you tried to stop it because of what your mind told you. And people do react when you are being yourself, both positively and negatively. But often people don't really notice us or judge us, regardless of the condition we are in. They may be afraid or jealous or envious, or maybe they learn from you. If one person feels a connection to reality because of you and feels more authentic, it is worth much of the trouble we have to go through.

Student: Thank you.

Karen: I had a little sign on my refrigerator for a long time that said, "I'd rather be disliked for something that I am than loved for something that I am not." Let them not like you. Somebody will find you and say, "What a jewel."

Student: Thank you.

Karen: And there is a chance that they will. But don't wait until then to be yourself.

Student: I'm a newcomer here, and perhaps you will not like what I want to say. What came up in our inquiry was anger. And it turned out that it was anger that I had yesterday. We got clear about it, so I want to speak out here. I want to start by saying that I was so happy this morning when you spoke those words out of a woman's sensibility. Yesterday I was really pissed off with Hameed's talk. I know he is here, so I am also addressing him. I also was pissed off with you because you spoke only like a man. I was feeling that there are so many women who have been abused and are still abused by this energy, and I did need the word "respect." I did not hear it one time. It is wonderful to say as a man to a man, "Go for it." I also want my lover to go for it—but with respect.

I needed that because I would like to remember that eros, this energy, the kundalini, is a snake in the beginning, a reptile. And then it moves through other parts of us, through the heart, and then it changes, as you said, in such a lovely way. I was very touched by what you said. Also when you said, "I want to be naked in my soul before your naked soul . . ." So I thank you for that.

Karen: Thank you for being willing to say you are pissed off.

Student: Thank my partner, who said, "Go for it" and encouraged me to stand up, because there are people like me who do not clap and who are all sitting very quiet, well-behaved, while there are unexpressed feelings.

Karen: What are you feeling right now?

Student: I feel energy.

Karen: Feeling a little heat, too, aren't you?

Student: Much heat.

Karen: That's actually one of the beautiful things about being able to deal with our aggression in a responsible way. We don't act it out or repress it. Anger can lead to that creative force and energy and fire. And it's neither male nor female. It is an aspect of what we are. Go, girl!

9

Magnetic Love

HAMEED

WE HAVE BEEN INQUIRING into and exploring divine eros as a force, as an energy that helps us to connect with and recognize the unity, the nonduality, of reality. When we recognize the depth, the absolute nature, of ourselves—of everything—we see that one particular thing that characterizes it is its unity. We recognize reality as one, single and indivisible, and this unites us all in a much deeper way than we anticipate . . . or like to anticipate.

The unity of our true nature has many facets, many kinds of depth, and many meanings. It is a unity in many ways, one of which is the oneness, the nonduality, of external forms and the ground of our true nature. Another way is the unity between us as individuals—that we are not separate. That is why, when we chant HU, the secret name of our absolute nature, our ultimate nature, we want to hear it from everywhere . . . because it *is* everywhere. So we hear ourselves saying it, we hear other people saying it and, if we really become absorbed in the sound and the intimacy of it, the sound itself can take us to the unity. It is possible to recognize as we hear the various voices chanting the sound HU, that not only are we in unison, but it is the unity sounding as many voices. And the unity is expressing itself as one sound, as it is one manifestation.

So sound is one way of experiencing the oneness of manifestation. We are part of one sound; our sound is part of the one sound. As we do this, we are participating in the one sound—the absolute nature saying its own name through all of us, because that's who says it anyway, always and at all times. We think that it is we who are saying it, but actually it is our deepest nature saying it . . . which turns out to be who we are at the deepest level.

Uniting Animal and Angel

It feels very nice here, very sweet. I can tell that many people are feeling their heart open. It is nice to feel the field of the group.

Many teachings enable us to realize the unity of Being. And there are many ways to reach or recognize the nondual condition, the primordially natural condition of our Being and our consciousness. Our approach here is that of uniting the animal and the angel, our animal nature and our angelic or divine nature. Human beings possess the potential to integrate these two parts of ourselves even though we begin as animals. That is, we begin life as babies with the animal drive dominant, and our animal nature continues to be a very important part of us. No matter how much we want to disown our animal aspect, it is not possible, because we are animal in our physicality.

Divine eros is a topic that invites the purity of our spiritual nature to combine with the power of our animal instinct. Instinct is animal, and "animal" generally means "primitive." The animal in us is a powerful primitive force that humanity still hasn't learned to deal with in a completely human way. Consequently, we have many fears and many conflicts about experiencing desire and its erotic expression.

We have fears about the erotic just as we have fears about love. Love is very scary because of how vulnerable we are when we feel it, how undefended, how delicate. But our erotic side, our desire, brings in the animal part of our nature. Our fear about that is partly due to the possibility of rejection by or the loss or unavailability of the other. Yet desire is also a force that can bring us in touch with our sense of power. This can feel good and, conversely, it can bring out our aggression, our anger, and our hatred, which we might be afraid of.

We can also be scared of the desire and aggression of other people toward us if we show our excitement, our heart, or our desire. So inner conflict can just as easily be stimulated by other people wanting and desiring us.

Dealing with either love or desire can bring up strong feelings of resistance and defensiveness, along with many other emotions, conflicts, beliefs, and ideas, as well as much of our own personal history. In particular, when we get what we want—or what we don't want—in the territory of love or desire, what is often evoked is pain, difficulty, and frustration.

The Distortion of Eros

The story of eros in human history has not been exactly wonderful. The sexual component of eros—sexual desire and interest—has been misused in various ways. Sexual energy and its various expressions have led to abuse through addiction, attachment, indulgence, and spiritual ignorance; but more significantly, it has led to abuse through aggression and violence. For many people, eros has meant a lot of domination, cruelty, and violent behavior. Many of us have a history of being forced to deal with inappropriate behavior and have often had overwhelming experiences related to our sexuality, such as rape. Hence, as we discuss and explore the various dimensions of eros, we tend to encounter those memories, that pain, and that history—both our own and that of other people.

As I said at the beginning of this seminar, our culture has only recently been learning how to value relationship, how to value being sensitive with one another, how to recognize other people as precious, as important, as having their own sensitivity, as being their own center of awareness. The issues of relationship and personalness, of contact, attunement, and empathy, have been introduced here in order to situate eros within that context. That is why we are exploring divine eros, not just eros.

For most of humanity, the experience of eros is usually superficial, insensitive, or even nonexistent. So discussing the intensity, the passion, or the power of eros can bring up the feeling, "Oh, this can be dangerous." Our own intensity can feel dangerous or our history might include other people's passion being dangerous for us. We hear about that danger in the news, from our friends, in our families. As we do our work here, it is fine that these memories, emotions, and associations come up. We want to explore them and welcome them because inquiry is inclusive of all our experience. We embrace all of ourselves, because if we let all of our feelings and experiences be, if we hold them with curiosity and interest, they will become keys to unlocking the luminous manifestations of who we are. Our understanding of them brings forth the luminosity that can take our experience deeper into unity.

Almost everything that we explore can be experienced by a part of us as a threat. We can discuss sweetness or love, but for many of us those seem to be dangerous possibilities, just as tenderness and empathy can be. For many of us, desire and wanting are dangerous. The same is true about sexuality. Union, to which many of us aspire, can seem full of danger. "Unity . . . wow, that means I am going to die!"

Unity sounds like a lofty and noble spiritual condition, but for the normal mind, it is very threatening. So if you are experiencing resistance, contraction, tension, trembling, anger, hurt, wounding, frustration, disappointment, or loss, that is absolutely fine. It is expected. These are the things that we need to metabolize, understand, and move through in order to activate within us—and to feel comfortable with—our eros in a divine way, in a way that expresses its essential nature.

Our understanding of eros is that its true essence is beautiful and wonderful. But when the erotic expresses itself in destructive ways, then it is not solely erotic. It is vulgar and distorted; something else has been added to it. True eros is not separate from love, and by studying it in this teaching as divine eros, we are attempting to demonstrate that. There is only one eros and it is always truly divine, but we do not always experience it in its purity. We experience it mixed with our frustration, with our history, with our dissociation, with our anger or revenge or hurt, and so it comes out unclear and twisted. That is why, for many people, it becomes abusive, it becomes destructive, it becomes insensitive.

This situation is similar to what we see when we observe most human beings. Our true nature as human beings is our spiritual nature, and it is pure and complete goodness, but you wouldn't know that by looking around the world and studying the history of humanity. In fact, you'd wonder whether the theory of the goodness of human nature is valid. There is not much proof that it is; examples everywhere tend to demonstrate the opposite. But the nature of the erotic is also this pure and complete goodness. When we know eros for what it truly is, it will be expressed in beautiful ways, just like when a human being is really expressing his or her true nature.

UNITY: TWO AS ONE

Unity is an interesting concept. It has little scientific basis and there is no basis for it in history. We see more movement toward separation and fragmentation than toward unity. We have more countries in the world today than we did fifty years ago, which in some sense is good, but it is also a movement toward increasing separation. Everybody wants to be themselves, and it seems that we have to be separate from one another to do that. We don't know how to be ourselves and be connected at the same time. It is not easy. That is why we have been discussing here the importance of realizing our autonomy. That is why we are exploring our need to feel stable and secure in our sense of who we are in order to freely experience the desire for union, or to experience the unity itself. Otherwise, we will feel threatened.

So how can we have unity while everybody retains his or her

autonomy and uniqueness? How can unity and uniqueness coexist for the individual? This is something that the European Union is trying to work out, and it is a struggle, as you have noticed. Things move forward a little and then take a step back. We want unity, but everybody says, "No, I want my own culture; my national identity will disappear if we merge." That is natural. That is how human beings are.

Unity feels so threatening because it eliminates separateness—not only duality but separateness. When we experience complete unity, we feel it as the depth of our heart, as our purest identity. When we know who we are without any distraction, without any ideas, without any influences—when we are completely free being ourselves and knowing ourselves exactly for what we are, directly and immediately—we recognize that what we are is the unity of the universe. This unity is the one from which many come, but this one is also very scary, because we feel that there are not many, not three, not two, only one. In fact, it is not even one. It is the One that is not a number, the One that is not the opposite of two or many. It is the One that is everything, the One without any other. That is why the scary thing about this unity is that it is not different from zero. But at the same time, it is the most intimate we can be in our experience—the deepest, the most sincere, the most genuine, the most truthful.

This One is an absolute authenticity and realness that has no size at all, no shape. And it is our very center, but when we look, we realize that it is your center, and my center, and his center, and her center, and everybody's center. It is one, single, and it has no size. It is not a thing, so when we say "One" in this sense, we don't mean one thing. This is a mysterious truth, paradoxical, and, for many of us, it doesn't make sense.

We might be scared of it, but when we feel it, it is the most beautiful, satisfying truth. It is the unity beyond time and space. What we are is beyond time and space. "Beyond time" means it doesn't have time. "Beyond space" means it doesn't have space. Unity doesn't have duration—length of time—and it doesn't have distance—depth in space. So it is timeless and spaceless, but it appears as all time and all space. It includes and is the source of time and space but is also beyond it. It is independent of time and space; in fact, time and space are dependent on it in order to exist in our perception and experience.

Because this deep and satisfying truth is independent in this way, and because it is what we are, when we know it we know that we are here in *this* place but also that we are there in *that* place. While we are there, the "there" is "here"; it is not over there. "There" exists only in the language of time and space. In the language of truth, nothing is "there"—it is all "here." I can only give you approximations that point us to the truth that is inclusive and beyond these concepts. There is not even a "here," because "here" is a word that implies the concept of space. The point is that there is no "here" and no "there." The unity we are discussing is absolute, for there is neither time nor space that can separate one thing from another, you from me. We are the same—not two expressions of the same, but the same.

If the ultimate truth is such a unity, such singleness, which is actually a singularity, what will the impact be as we begin to be touched by it, as we begin to open to that truth, as we come closer to it? How will we feel its effect on us? Using the conventional language of time and space, we would say, "I am here and you are there." But since neither of us feels any distance, it seems as though a magnet were pulling us toward each other. We feel that we are one, but we perceive two, and the result is that we both feel a force bringing us together. And the closer we are, the more powerfully we will feel it. Just like two magnets: When they are relatively far from each other, there is some attraction, but the closer they get, the more powerful the attraction becomes. What do the magnets want to do? They want to become so connected that they are one, for one is the truth. Twoness is ultimately appearance, not reality. More accurately, it is simply how reality appears, not what it fundamentally is.

The Attraction Called Love

This truth is beyond our comprehension, but it manifests in our hearts as the force we call love. Love wants you to be closer to the one you love. Don't you notice that when you like somebody, you want to spend more time with him or her? The more you like that person, the closer you feel you want to be, and the more time you want to spend together. Have you ever heard of anybody who falls in love and says, "I want to go away . . . I don't want to see you"? Actually, that does happen, but only if you get scared to come too close. You start out feeling, "I want to be so close that I won't want to go away," but that can become too threatening: "If that happens, I'll never go to work again. Who is going to take care of things?"

But love has many degrees, many dimensions, and is of many kinds, depending on how close we are to the mystery of truth, the mystery of unity. This mystery of unity has been described as pure light, as enlightenment, as total peace, freedom, purity, perfection. Whatever it is, we are trying to enlist the mystery of unity to help us arrive at that unity by seeing how it emerges in our experience, how its reflection appears in our everyday life. We feel it as a love, as a liking, an attraction that makes us want to get closer. We also feel it as the desire to be closer to what we desire.

This attraction is a central expression of life. On the animal level, life is very intelligent. It has learned to use this force of coming together in order to ensure that life reproduces, survives, and continues. What more powerful force than the pull toward pleasurable union can biological life use to continue its existence? Animals do it. Birds do it. Bees do it. Humans do it. They all like it because the power of that mystery is being used, appearing in biological life as the erotic instinct.

Initially, this force appears biologically as the desire to come together to continue the race, to continue life. This desire begins as a drive of life for life, and then, in the human being, develops to become a desire not just to reproduce the species but as a more conscious desire to come together, to be close, to be intimate, to be unified, to experience the unity. Human beings have the capacity to know this unity. Life is intelligent, as we know, because it is expressing the intelligence of mysterious nature itself. It is evolving so that the mystery can come to know itself more completely.

Life first begins to reveal its mystery in primitive, biological ways, then advances to the level of the emotions, and ultimately appears in mystical union itself, consciously. This unity is more than the joining of bodies; the physical unity of intercourse is merely an approximation of something far more intimate. That is why the unity we are talking about requires so much maturity. It requires much development, much refinement, for human beings to appreciate that the erotic encounter is not just for pleasure, not just to have orgasm, but to experience the exquisiteness of contact, of intimacy, to experience the bliss of coming to know the mystery together. By coming together, we are able to know the unity of reality. When divine eros consummates, we are helping each other to know this deepest of all mysteries. But the intimacy of union does not have to be sexual, because the unity is beyond the physical, beyond time and space.

MAGNETISM: THE PULL OF DIVINE UNITY

We are working with, exploring, and arriving at this truth through the magnetic force instead of through a technique, a meditation, or a traditional practice that is not part of our lives. There are many good ways to arrive at that truth, and all of them can work. But we're focusing on a particular way that can be useful in our everyday life. We don't just want to experience the mystery of unity; we want to know it in a way that enhances our life, that makes our life more complete, more human, that can bring our humanity to fruition, to a ripening.

What most of us know of eros is an approximation of the essential spiritual condition of feeling true magnetism, the true attraction that many of us feel in relationship to the divine, in relationship to God, in relationship to truth, in relationship to the absolute, in relationship to our true nature. We feel drawn to it. We feel pulled toward it. We feel attracted to it. We can experience it as an interest, as a longing, as a desire, as a determination. But when we finally know it, we feel it as a force, a magnetic gravitational force, pulling our soul in a direction that we don't know but can't help moving toward. And when we feel that attraction in our heart, we feel it as a kind of love, as the subtlest kind of love. Love always wants to bring us closer to what we love, whether the object of love is God, truth, or reality, whether it is a car, an iPad, or a person.

There is a natural magnetism toward the unity, the unity between our true nature and our individual consciousness. Sometimes we feel this attraction as an interest, as a gravitational pull toward the unity, and sometimes as a love or need for it. We feel drawn to it, driven toward it, and at times we also feel it as a mutual attraction. It is not only that we are attracted to truth—the truth is attracted to us. Not only are we attracted to God, God is attracted to us. We are pulled toward God, and God is pulled toward us. The two are drawn together because they are one at the center. Some teachings think of God as totally separate from the human soul, but in true mystical union, at least in the way we are discussing here, such separation evaporates, in one way or another. In the type of unity we are exploring, there is no possibility of such a separation.

When our love becomes very refined, very pure, very subtle, when it is at its subtlest, purest, most delicate—which requires total vulnerability, with no defensiveness—we recognize it explicitly as a magnetic love. Not only do you feel "I love you," but when you say, "I love you," you cannot help but feel drawn as the words are spoken. You feel a magnetic force that can only be felt as a wanting or desire. And the desire is not for the other; it is for unity with the other.

This is usually easier to feel in relation to our spiritual ground— with God or with true nature. When we become aware of that level of heart, we have found one of the deepest possible motivations for spiritual work, one of the most effective reasons to engage the inner journey. And because of that powerful force, we feel we can't help it—we need to go there, we have to go there, we want to go there, we love to go there. We want to be as close to the truth as possible, so close that we don't exist anymore . . . only the truth exists.

One important reason why we are learning about divine eros is so that we can recognize and better understand this force within us, in our psyche, in our soul. This force can become a powerful motive and a motivational power that can help us with the difficult task of spiritual work. As we have seen, there are many difficulties, many barriers and obscurations on the inner path. These emotions, feelings, and memories are simply the obstacles in the way of recognizing and living the unity. They are so many, so powerful, and so difficult, that we need a powerful force that is beyond our own volition, beyond our own choice; otherwise, we don't have much of a chance. If left to our own choice, we will choose to run away.

Magnetic love is appreciative, generous, selfless; it is a sweetness, a liking, a lovingness and tenderness and, at the same time, a magnetic pull that you can experience as wanting or desire. But it is more fundamental than desire or wanting. When you desire, you feel that you are doing something. Actually, something is controlling you from inside, pulling on you. You can feel it as "I am wanting," but it is not *you* who wants. It is the absolute that wants, through exerting its gravitational force. The truth wants to reveal itself, and you feel this as a relationship of love to the truth, as an interest or an attraction to it.

The Truth of Unity

For me, this love, this gravitational love for reality, is more powerful than the desire that the truth relieve my pain, my suffering. The desire to relieve suffering can be powerful but for many people, it is not sufficient. We don't even know how much pain we have. When we find that out, the desire for salvation from suffering—others' suffering and our own—will be immense. However, even the desire to relieve the pain is because of love. Compassion is one way love expresses itself; we want those whom we love to be happy and not suffer. The mystery itself, that mystery of unity, is pure, thrilling pleasure. It is a bursting kind of joy. It is very subtle, very quiet, but at the same time it is an intense, searing delight. It is the most intense ecstasy but the most quiet at the same time. It is complete undisturbed stillness, but because of its subtlety the most penetrating.

Understanding this magnetic force within us can help us clarify how to have a strong, powerful, deep motivation to continue to be real, to be as real as possible, to dedicate our time and life to experiencing, living, and expressing the truth, the truth of the mystery. Since this mystery is the truth of unity, its expression is love, generosity, and the experience of coming together in the most appreciative, sensitive way. Experienced from this perspective, the mystery itself, our true nature, is complete clarity, radiance, and brilliance. Also, this type of magnetism is pure luminosity. When we feel this luminosity in the heart, we feel it as the luminosity of magnetic love. It is beautiful, sublime. It feels so delicate, so fine, so refined, and so subtle, all at the same time; and although it is so subtle, its effect is of the most powerful, most passionate attraction.

Again, this is paradoxical. It doesn't make sense to the mind, because we think that something so subtle and so delicate should be fragile, not powerful. It is the subtlest kind of love, the barest kind of delicate, effervescent luminosity. But its impact is an amazing magnetic attraction that appears as a liking, as an enjoyment—as the enjoyment and the liking of love itself, of desire itself, of the pull itself, of the unity itself. This force, which is also exquisite love, can become the appreciation of our true nature, but it can also express itself as an attraction between people.

We get a whiff of that, a glimpse of that, when we fall in love, especially when two people fall in love at the same time. This is one of the few situations in normal life when we can feel this magnetic force. We want to be together at all costs, as close together as possible, as much of the time as possible. We want to go everywhere with our beloved at all times. What do you think that means? It means that we want to fill time and space completely, because that is what the experience of being in love is. The truth fills time and space, so you want to do everything together, all the time; you don't want to be separate.

But those feelings are like a little spark that doesn't remain very long because so much stuff is brought up and challenged by it—so much of our psyche, our unconscious, our history. It's like having a nuclear explosion underneath our unconscious; everything comes out and you have to deal with it. That is why the experience of being in love doesn't last very long for most people. The couple might continue to be loving with each other, but the pull, the irresistible magnetic attraction, doesn't stay strong because so much is in the way of it.

It is possible, though quite rare, for two people to feel this type of strong attraction continually, and to experience it as two individuals drawn to each other in the same way that magnets work: The closer you are to each other, the more powerful the attraction is. When that happens, there is no limit to how powerful the magnetism can be. It becomes like a singularity. In mathematics, a singularity occurs when the magnitude curve rises to infinity. "Singular" means "one," of course. As the power in the union of two individual souls approaches infinity, they recognize this singular nature as the one that they are. It is truly a marvelous, momentous occurrence.

Our hearts need to be very ripened to know the utmost possibility of human fruition. It takes a great deal of experience and understanding, and a great deal of wisdom, for us to tolerate that subtle, sweet luminosity that is the very essence of what brings things together. Perhaps when we come up with a mathematical representation of this, we will discover the unified field theory. It's an idea I have about what will make a unified field theory possible, since that is about the unifying of all natural forces. Although scientists are attempting to unify physical forces, for my theory to be plausible, they will likely have to discover a more basic force that underlies the presently known physical forces.

The type of love we are talking about doesn't differentiate between appreciation and desire, between love and eros, between the divine and the animal. That is why, when the soul has developed in a way that unifies the animal and the angel, we call it "the divine animal." Another expression for it is "the sexy angel." What is a sexy angel? It is a soul that is full of desire but it is still angelic, which means that it is pure, total light. It is the luminous force of the mystery of unity that all souls are looking for, and they are seeking it because it is driving them together with its magnetism. We might believe that we are searching, but in fact we are simply being attracted. The more that we feel we are not in control, the more fortunate we are.

We have discussed many things today: the force that brings us closer to unity, whether with the divine or with another person; the various difficulties that arise as this force touches us and stirs up memories, feelings, resistances, and tensions; all the fears about the desire or the love we experience in ourselves and others; the anger, aggression, and conflict that can arise. All of these are part of the process.

EXPLORATION SESSION

This exercise is ideally done with one or two partners. One at a time, each person will spend about fifteen minutes inquiring. You can also do it alone through writing. You will be looking into how you experience this magnetism, this magnetic love, this attraction toward reality, truth, God, or another person. You want to see how you experience it, how aware of it you are, how developed it is in you. You also want to explore what kinds of resistances or difficulties you recognize in yourself as you become more aware of it.

Note any of your reactions to the magnetism that are arising out of the exploration we have been doing. Explore those reactions. The more you recognize what they are, the more you can be free of them and the more possible it will be for you to access one of the purest motivating forces for enlightenment.

Another useful inquiry is to find out and to understand how much this force has become a motivation for you in your inner work—whether it is active in you as a motive for the inner journey.

Hopefully you will get some understanding of the role of that force as a motivation.

Student: Today when you spoke, I felt completely heartbroken. I desire unity with God and truth and myself, and I find that to feel such desire is not difficult; but to desire unity with humanity, with all human beings, is so difficult because of all the pain that I feel. I realized that I have felt that all my life, and that I have to separate myself and try to make this spot safe at least. When you talked, I thought, "I have to go to a monastery."

Hameed: It is obviously true that there is much pain in humanity. You are saying that to open to unity with humanity means to open to all that pain. This means to me, in some sense, that you are capable of feeling the pain of humanity. We might be afraid of that, but we usually feel only what we can tolerate, when it comes to this kind of empathic feeling. You don't have to push yourself in that direction. When your heart is big enough to hold it, that will happen; otherwise, it won't.

Student: When I was a child, I always prayed and asked, "Please, God, don't let me be crucified." I guess this is kind of the same feeling.

Hameed: To feel humanity's pain will feel like being crucified.

Student: Yes.

Hameed: There is a lot of pain . . . it might actually be worse than being crucified. Humanity's pain is tremendous, but our heart is actually bigger. Feeling the pain of humanity is not what most people think it is. When you feel somebody else's pain, for instance, usually you can feel it because you can hold it; you have the capacity to experience it. This requires an amazing depth of sensitivity; otherwise, we don't feel it, we just know that they have pain. But it seems you are afraid of it because you imagine you might possibly feel the pain of all humanity. The pain of humanity, even though it is big, is not the biggest thing about humanity. When I feel one with humanity, the pain is on the surface and is a small part of what humanity is.

Humanity is mostly life, creativity, intelligence, and many other wonderful things. There is much pain and much aggression, but in seeing how humanity endured and flourished, you might get an intuition of the tremendous intelligence within its soul.

Student: It's like you have to go through the pain.

Hameed: You have to be willing to feel the pain—that is true.

Student: I just want to thank you so much for your books. Every day, I feel like I am a child taken by the hand and shown the way, and I am so grateful. Thank you.

Hameed: Glad to hear that the books have been useful for you. That is the intention behind them.

Student: I don't feel the same way, even after reading your books. This is not to offend you . . . but that is the very strange thing in my experience.

I can feel the magnetism in some way, and it is very strong, but I have no clue of direction. With force, there should be a direction. That is a definition of force—that it has power and direction. But I don't feel the direction, and that is very strange.

Hameed: If you feel magnetism, you are feeling pulled.

Student: Toward it.

Hameed: How do you experience that feeling of being pulled?

Student: Like being pulled inside out, like losing all ground. It's also like this: When I get closer I don't know anything anymore. It is like it has no face. When I get closer, it loses its face.

Hameed: When you feel it, you don't know anything; is that difficult?

Student: It's very pleasant. So what is my question?

Hameed: Maybe that is the direction. Not-knowing might be a good direction. It seems that it's pulling you. Nobody knows the direction. You don't know where the magnet is because it is everywhere. It is not going to pull you in one direction or another. It is going to pull you toward itself, and that will make you feel that finally you are getting closer and dissolving into some kind of mystery. One of the ways this manifests is that you don't know what's going on—and this not-knowing feels delicious. So just let yourself stay with the not-knowing—that you don't know anything. Just feel it and be there.

Student: I tried that for a few years, but it should end somewhere. But I understand your answer.

Hameed: The force doesn't pull you in a direction, in the usual meaning of the word "direction." It pulls you toward itself, so it takes you deeper, it takes you closer, to more mystery, though not necessarily in a particular recognizable spatial direction. And when we talk about a path, we don't mean that it is something you can visualize. These words are not to be taken literally.

Student: This is my question, also. I have no idea where to go or what to do.

Hameed: If you stay with that not-knowing, you will see what happens. That will be a good direction. It is normal to feel disoriented, because we are challenging the usual orientation to your experience. We are offering a different approach.

Student: While listening to your teaching, there was an attraction and also, in my body, there was stress building up. And during the inquiry, what arose was a poem [by the Dutch poet P. N. van Eyck] called "Death and the Gardener," and what I realize from that poem is that the attraction is everywhere. Now I feel there is relaxation in my body. Maybe I built up stress to be like the gardener, so that I can go away from it, but it is everywhere. And it relaxed me to see that it is not necessary anymore to go away from it, because when I go away from it, it is there, too. It is relaxing to stay here.

Hameed: It is true. You can't get away from it, because it is not in time or space.

Student: So I will write a poem for myself.

Hameed: Even when we say "go deeper," we think of the depth of an ocean. That is still space. "Deeper" means "more experientially deeper." It is not going anywhere. It is just where you are; you become what it is.

―――――――――

Student: I want to share a reconciliation that I somehow forgot, which happened with the magnetic force. I spent quite some time in several ashrams and monasteries and I had this feeling like I really want to know the truth; I really want to love God. I felt pulled by this love of God and, at the same time, a lot of doubts were there: "Is this a kind of escape? Shouldn't I stay here in Europe and not go to India?" The inquiry and your talk reconciled me with this drive I am experiencing, by making me more clear. It is not a kind of escape but really an ecstatic drive I am experiencing.

At the same time, another thing became clear, which is that sometimes in experiencing sexuality, I feel something is missing. It has been frustrating, and I could never really clarify what it is. Listening to you, it became clear to me that these are somehow the same forces that are driving me; this force of unity is not only on the physical level; they go far beyond what I have thought. I feel very relieved and glad.

Hameed: It is relieving. When we are young, when we are adolescent teenagers, physical sex seems great, wonderful, all the way throughout. However, as we mature—and mature doesn't mean just get old, it means we have more understanding, more sensitivity—we realize that the physical is not enough, because it needs a deeper dimension for it to be complete.

―――――――――

Student: During your lecture, I started feeling very touched about the things you said, especially about the soft quietness of our nature, our spiritual nature. During the inquiry, I started to listen to this very, very soft call. It was like the answering was coming, and it came very powerfully. I thought I couldn't stand it because it touched me so powerfully, for there was no doubt in it. There was absolute trust that it would find me. I had to do nothing. It was like, "Okay, you are hearing me, and now I will come." I'm absolutely sure and absolutely straight and really powerful, but what you said about this softness felt really amazing.

Normally I think that you are talking about things I will never experience, and when other people say similar things here, I think, "Okay, maybe they have read it in your books." But now I am feeling these things. It is a new experience for me.

Hameed: So you had a good taste of what we are exploring.

Student: Yes, I had a really good taste. For me, laughing and crying are very close together in this experience. I just had to laugh when the other people were saying something . . . I don't know how to say it in English. I am very thankful; I got a taste of this . . . I would call it an energy that I could not doubt, which touched me really deeply.

Hameed: When you feel touched by the truth that way, there is no doubt. The mind becomes still.

Student: So thank you very much.

Hameed: Sometimes you read the books and sometimes you don't read the books! You can be touched either way. Truth is everywhere, not just in the books.

––––––––––––––––––––

Music Meditation

Suggested Selection:

"Noche Gaditana," from the album *Suite Andalouse* by Pedro Soler and Renaud Garcia-Fons

As you listen to the music, you want to feel your heart. You can experience it and see it as a window to your inner beloved, to your true nature, to reality, to God—whatever name you want to use. It is like an open window that opens to that mysterious reality. Let the music open your heart further to various feelings and attitudes that may arise.

10

Sexy Angel

KAREN

IT HAS BEEN QUITE A JOURNEY. Our hope is that you have had a taste of the divine and found some sparkling thread that you have been able to follow inward to the understanding of divine eros. Divine eros will manifest in your body, your relationships, and your life as you understand it more fully.

We also hope that you will be able to keep doing the practices we have been working with, so that they can nourish and support a greater freedom in you. Meditation is a very important foundation for inquiry. In our lives, we get thrown to the surface of our experience, to the usual conventional view. The conventional consciousness of the world has the compelling perspective that the physical dimension is the most fundamental; hence, there is a gravitational pull away from presence. Even though we have experience to the contrary, we tend to take on this perspective unwittingly and find ourselves empty, deficient, wanting, often forgetting what it was that we truly love and want. We forget about the silence, the depth, the joy and lightness of Being. So it is important to make time in your daily life to reconnect to yourself.

You will all go back into your usual life now. It is important to know that what we have been experiencing here is not separate from your daily life, even though we have held a stronger focus on the inner dimensions. You do not want to separate what you have learned here from your daily existence, because that will divide your heart once again.

The Importance of Continued Practice

If you apply what you have learned here, it can take you a very long way inward. It would be very gratifying for us to know that you are diligent in staying with the practices and remembering what you love—we trust that you will find yourself growing as a result.

That is the basis of discipline: You do something because you love it. You feel the rightness of it. That helps you to remember your intention to practice and to persevere in following through on that intention. If the heart doesn't feel that something is right for you, you can't do it. You won't feel the motive for it. When you know it's the right thing for you, you sit to meditate, inquire, and attend to yourself through practice; you find the time because you want to, even if it is difficult. You stay in touch with your belly and, over time, your belly starts calling you, starts rumbling when you are not paying enough attention. At some point, it sends out a message: "Hello . . . Hey! Down here . . ." You become more sensitive to your condition and feel both the connection and the disconnection from Being more distinctly.

Practice increases presence and awareness in depth and intensity, and as your presence expands and becomes more accessible, you become more aware of its absence. Developing presence in the belly creates a center of gravity for Being, so that the perspective of the world doesn't take you into its gravitational pull as strongly. That doesn't mean you won't forget, but over time, with the awakening of this center, you will become more grounded in Being. Developing this capacity for grounding begins with taking the time to do the practices you have been taught. Over time, you will see the benefits, and the center of gravity you develop will allow you to stay in touch with a deeper reality throughout the various situations in your life. In taking your practice seriously, you will be able to feel a greater capacity to follow through on your intention to be in touch with yourself, whatever state you may be in, and to be real, regardless of the condition you find yourself in and the content that life brings your way.

As a result, you develop presence as a normal part of life's expression. At the same time, you feel drawn inward; you feel the attraction to the silence, the source of your Being. The love for that silence, luminosity, and equanimity grows, and it becomes your sanctuary.

The situation of our inner life is similar to what happens when we first fall in love. Magnetic love needs time to develop. When you are in courtship, when you haven't completely fallen in love yet, you need to spend the time to get to know somebody, don't you? You tell yourself, "Well, maybe I'll say yes to that second or third date . . . Yeah, I do like him." Once a person has caught your interest and the magnetism attracts you, you *want* to do the things that are necessary to nourish the relationship. Now you want to spend the time it takes to do that.

When you are called by something inner—something beyond your usual awareness—and you begin to practice, at some point you may begin to notice the impact of that something. You feel awe as you taste the freedom, and if you truly value it, you sense that it's important enough to pay attention to in a more consistent way. The inward pull begins to gather significance and momentum that gets stronger and stronger until you can't take your mind off it and can't keep your heart from being absorbed in it. Should you forget about it, you feel the disconnection, dissatisfaction, and, eventually, the pain of that. The yearning becomes a sign that you are swerving from the path, from what you love, which in turn brings you back to the presence of the Beloved you have turned away from.

So, if you really apply yourself to the practices and allow the energy of desire to guide you, this will open you more to the inner

Beloved, whether or not you ever attend another event or read another book that's considered spiritual. It is difficult to follow the path completely on your own, but you can still do much for yourself.

The practices you have learned here will help you to go beyond the usual level of experience. You cannot establish your inner orientation with the mind, but the heart knows when you are headed in the right direction. The mind becomes quieter. This doesn't mean that you get stupid; in becoming still, the mind opens to a new dimension of itself to assist the heart on the quest for truth, so we venture into unknown territory and begin to learn to know in new ways. Our desire is not only to feel the truth but also to know it completely and to be taken in by it totally. With its innate intelligence and capacity for discrimination, the mind works in partnership with the heart. The heart with its love is what stirs within the soul and makes us want to be nearer. The heart is what feels closeness and distance. The love is what melts the boundaries and awakens the soul to her Beloved and the desire for union with the divine. And the mind plays the important role of discriminating the experience and clarifying the consciousness through understanding.

To truly know our nature, we need to be and know it fully, and at some point we realize that we cannot separate the two. To know Being is to be it. To be it is to feel it and know it as one unified phenomenon. Then the heart and mind are united in their action and function. The heart says, "Yes, I love you." The mind says, "I want to completely know what I love." It is not enough simply to be in love and feel the love. You want to know what you love. You love to know what you love.

When you fall in love with somebody, you want to know what kind of cereal he eats. You want to know if she prefers chocolate or vanilla. "Are you interested in physics?" "Do you like to exercise?" "What kind of music do you listen to?" "Where were you born?" "What was it like for you growing up?" You want to know everything. You want to explore every bit, inside and out, backward and forward. Love is a force that compels us to want to know more.

The heart is the beacon that shows us the way. Through the love for the truth, our direction is set as by an astrolabe. As we melt more completely into our experience, it is the mind that discriminates the truth and meaning of what we are experiencing. A looping between the heart and mind develops that reveals more and more levels of experience, meaning, and truth. The love and knowing create a synergistic effect that enables consciousness to continue beyond what we have known into indescribable universes of experience.

As you have all seen in our work together, we are able to speak the unspeakable and name our experience of the unnameable. Our mind and our heart work together, using our words to support the process rather than interfere with it. The beauty of speech in our practice is that we are able to use words as a tool, a vehicle to open to and carry the message and meaning of the invisible into the visible.

FROM CHARGE TO FREEDOM

One thing you have learned that will be very useful in your lives is how to handle a reaction to someone or some situation when you notice that you are having it. It is important to allow that reaction, feel it, and at the same time to not act on it. Do not act out on that emotional charge, and don't suppress it either. Be aware of it and, when you can, inquire into it in order to understand it. See what the truth of your experience is. You can be in it, feel it, and let it open up—whether it is anger, disgust, disappointment, agitation, or even positive feelings of joy and pleasure—and then follow the energy back to its origins.

Have you ever noticed that emotions have an energetic charge? Any kind of reactivity has a charge to it. When you allow yourself to be with your emotional charge, the feelings can open to new and deeper experiences if you approach them with interest and openness. Emotions can trap, distort, and limit the energy and thereby limit our experience when we do not approach them in the right way. Liberating the energy of our emotions liberates our consciousness.

As you have experienced in opening to this teaching, strength and aliveness arise within anger; tenderness and gentleness are awakened through sadness, and so on. Being in a field of spiritual inquiry, you can open to new levels of experience with only a small amount of encouragement and guidance. Approaching your experience in a different way than usual—by suspending your ideas and beliefs—opens up new potentials. And through understanding what the emotional charge was about and staying with it, you can see how it deepens your experience and releases the energy that was held inside the emotions.

Ideas, history, associations, and beliefs will all arise, but if we stay present and allow ourselves to continue to question and discriminate what is happening in the moment, then the content of what we are hurt by, feeling angry about, or disappointed in becomes clarified. Through understanding, we distill consciousness, in a sense, and are left with a purity, presence, energy. Sometimes we may recognize the loss of our connection to our nature, which can arise as a feeling of emptiness or of something lacking. In allowing this loss and the attendant feelings of grief and longing, we might discover and reconnect to the quality of Being that the emotion was cloaking, along with the liberated energetic dynamism of our aliveness.

The charge in our emotional experience is part of that thread of aliveness. Distortion of our true aliveness becomes emotional energy. If you clarify that emotion and you feel the energy of it, it becomes an energetic propulsion that drives you deeper into the real. This is the tantric way—don't express, don't suppress, just be with it. We are saying neither yes nor no to it; we are simply interested in understanding our experience: What is it? What does it mean? We want to discern the meaning and penetrate to the very last detail. As we discern and understand, the unshackled energy allows the process to unfold and take new forms.

In this way, through practice, we deepen back to the source and become a conduit for its expression. What begins as the release of emotional charge at the surface level of our existence becomes the entry into the freedom of continuous energetic renewal of our nature into manifestation. The ebb and flow of our consciousness is the expression of the pulse of life. The more you sense your belly and the more present you can be when you're having reactions or experiences of any kind, the more any experience can be an opening to the underlying stillness with its intelligent, creative dynamism.

The energy that transports and transforms us is the radiance of the silent stillness, which enables our life to take new form. We are born anew each moment, coming forward as radiance and purity, void of the reactive self based on the past. We are free in such a condition. This is a process that continues infinitely—individual consciousness in a continual, alive embrace with presence and emptiness, looping and spiraling as one living vortex, continually clarifying and purifying, learning and emptying, wanting and loving, blending and disappearing and rising again.

This process is not a matter of getting to an ultimate end or any particular state, where you say, "Okay, I get to my stillness or the dynamism and I'm done." No, over and over again, we're taken in and are birthed into Being once more in novel ways. This potential is true and present within all experience. Whatever your experience is, whatever is happening, there is freedom to be discovered within it. This is the discovery of the life of a real human being.

THE FOUR SPIRITUAL CENTERS

Our communion with our true nature expresses itself in perpetual *yabyum*—a loving embrace in which our energetic creative force and the stillness of Being are present as two sides of the same thing. The physical world and the spiritual world are not two; the interpenetration of these two sides is at each point of manifestation. The expression through our individual consciousness of this living being that we are can occur in many ways, and with many qualities. This is the preciousness of being human. We can know the secret of our nature within every atom of our Being, including our body. Our lives can be the conscious expression of the unity of Being, the spaciousness and total openness of what is.

The embodied human consciousness has four spiritual centers that are necessary for life. They are inborn as potentials for all human beings, but they do not develop or activate without the correct attitude and practices.

The first is the belly center, which has to do with the physical body and the embodiment of our presence. It is also the center responsible for action and movement. The second, the heart, in the center of the chest, is the seat of our feelings and the conduit of the love energy, sensitivity, and personal contact. Our mind is the third center, which is the discerning intelligence. The fourth center is located over the head and outside of the physical body. When the first three centers have opened and developed, and they function together in a balanced way, the fourth is ignited, which means that the conduit of the individual consciousness is awake to itself as Living Being manifesting in human form. It is said that when the fourth center opens, our real life has begun to be lived.

When these four centers are developed and impregnated with presence, our individual consciousness becomes radiant and functionally refined. The Russian mystic George I. Gurdjieff uses the concept of three centers and refers to them as three brains. Each of these develops a certain way of processing information. Each center is an organ of perception and expression. As living organisms, we have heart, mind, and belly, which are all differentiations of our consciousness that are needed for being in the world. They arise in particular ways and are in varying degrees of development in each one of us. We become like a prism for the deepest secret to live its life, refracting the light in specific and individual expressions of that secret for worldly functioning. So you are the secret one living the secret life! Right in front of everyone! This is the condition of the complete human being who is fully in the world of time and space yet not of it. This is the one who is the living, breathing secret name of God.

The four centers make you, in a sense, an organ of perception for God. You become the functioning mind, heart, and body of God. Your eyes see with the purity of perception; your ears hear the celestial hum within all of manifest reality; your nose opens to the sublime scents of existence; your fingers touch the texture of reality; you taste the richness in the diversity of life; you walk with the grace of eternity; you move with the totality of your nature. You are the individual consciousness that enables the universe to know and experience itself in varied ways.

Relationships become a playground for encounters that open up the potential for new experience, and our own pleasures as well as difficulties transform into opportunities for deeper contact. Our daily life can become an open field of discovery. When we know ourselves as the openness of Being, we are authentic in the truest sense of the word. Authentic not just because we can say, "This is really how I feel"—no, I mean "authentic" in the sense that we are real because we are the expression of the presence of the realness of our nature. We are the expression of that which makes everything real and allows anything to exist. Authenticity means being the depth of what we are and expressing it in as true a way as we can.

Integrating It All into One

Divine eros is the energy of communion and consummation. It inspires our consciousness to become one with our nature in complete interpenetration, where the silent stillness, the awake, lucid radiance, and the love intertwine in delicious intimacy. In the context of daily life, we can feel many combinations of these elements of consciousness. We can be quiet and still in the sanctuary of the deep or we can come forth and celebrate that depth in myriad ways. We taste and touch and feel it, palpably through encountering life and the infinite experiences it offers. We grapple with our inner conflicts and with other people, get through those, open up to something new. But it is not only struggles that open us, it is encountering any experience with openness to learn, and by doing so we end up with new and unending potential for experience. We can have no complete life without one another. And there is no real life without knowing the One.

The polarity of heaven and earth come together in the heart as the birth of divine eros—a living, breathing, pulsating, exuberant, aliveness that develops in us the personal beingness that has the capacity to be everything or nothing at all; we awaken to the whole, wide range of all possibilities. What seem to be polarity and opposites in the world of duality are, in the world of divine expression, only different expressions of the same thing. There is one love, one desire, one world, one home; and when we know this, we see this world as the face of our Beloved. The world becomes the expression and the body of our Beloved. That is just the appearance, of course, but if we really look, we see the Beloved shining through. It is that, too, in all its majestic radiance.

When we know freedom, we are able to be completely human, embracing our divine, physical, feeling, and thinking natures—all of who we are. Our nature is one undivided unity. Everything is that One. As true human beings, we are awake to the One that is all and everything, and simultaneously awake to the preciousness of our uniqueness inseparable from the oneness. No segmentation, no divisions, within or without. The heart, mind, and body appear as a unified whole that is functioning harmoniously as one unit inseparable from its deepest nature. As the unbounded vastness, we are the oneness coalescing in a particular place, within the world of time and space.

We are located, but that location does not define us nor does it separate us from one another or from the unity. We are individuated, differentiated forms of the unity . . . the wave of the ocean has matured to recognize its own unique expression of the oneness that it is. In our full humanness, we are the vehicle through which the vastness functions in time and space—seeing through our eyes, thinking through our mind, smelling through our nose, tasting through our mouth, feeling through our heart, and moving through our body.

As our heart matures into greater refinement, we become able to communicate with greater empathic skill, our body can become sensitive far beyond the physical level, and the mind becomes more open and bright, all of which enables us to live a mature life. We are increasingly more present and skilled in how we live our lives, how we deal with our relationships, how we do our work, how we spend our time. We become wise in our worldly actions and interactions. Wisdom is the great gift of embodied freedom.

This maturation and refinement make the divine prism that we are glow even more brightly with all the colors and all the beauty and radiance of our nature. Each facet is a luminous aspect of our nature, expressing the splendor of living being. We all have this potential and possibility to live and enjoy our lives while meeting life's challenges with increasing capacity and wisdom.

In this teaching we are not presenting a formal model of behavior that you should follow—for the simple reason that you can't decide to act like a complete human being; it is something that develops. But you can meet life's challenges with more heartfulness and more openness, as you go along. So it's not whether you have a reaction or not that makes you a developed human being; it's what you do with those reactions. It is not about what arises for you; it's about how you respond to what arises—that is the hallmark of maturity.

We make mistakes in our lives and in our relationships. We do our best not to, but we do cause pain sometimes. We also do things that enable people to experience great happiness. The point of practice is to apply in the best way you can what you know of the goodness of being, to learn from it and let it inform you and keep informing you. The truth is that people are going to have reactions to you regardless of how you appear. You can't avoid that. The more important question is about your own inner integrity. How do you feel in relation to yourself? How do you feel in relation to your inner nature, whether you perceive it as emptiness or the Beloved? And how do you feel in relationship to your Being and the energy that is your life? Are you making yourself available? Your Beloved is trying to seduce you at every moment. The natural seduction of the Beloved wants to take you inward. Within every experience is the Beloved, ready to awaken you, saying, "Here I am—just listen, look . . . and follow me."

Every reaction has within it the original pure energy that will optimize our evolution and our corporeal life. That pure energy is beckoning us. And the more we allow ourselves to be pulled by the One we love, the more that two people can meet as expressions of the One—two organs of perception peering into the vastness of each other's being.

What is possible for one's individual consciousness is also possible for the blended consciousness of two individuals—but with an amplified and intensified potentiality. Two as one can bring more variation of depth and breadth to the process of realization than is possible on one's own. You are able to see the Beloved in your partner and see your partner in yourself, like a hall of mirrors into the infinity of the infinite. You become a field of one, sensitive presence with the appearance of two, peering into the endless openness within one another.

As the magnetism of love influences our consciousness, drawing us into union, we become the divine incorporated into human form, naked to our nature and to our partner at the same time. The relational field can become the one appearing as two, and two creating a living vortex opening the one to new potential. This is at once the freedom of the openness of our nature expressed through the particularity of the relational field—erotic and divine, worldly and angelic. We are sexy angels!

Divine eros fulfills the spiritual quest as it fulfills human life, through the completion of the erotic life that can express itself in tantric relationships. When appropriate, such a relationship can be sexual, adding physical interpenetration, thus completing the cycle of relating. But as we have said, divine eros can animate (and enliven) any authentic human relationship.

You can take the knowledge of presence, the understanding of the relational field, and the skill of inquiry with you into your life. You can take all these jewels of wisdom with you wherever you go. This doesn't mean that you sit down with your lover, your partner, or your friend and say, "Okay, now we are going to do this thing called dialectic inquiry . . ." They won't know what you are talking about. But you can be as authentic as you can, simply by being more real in the interactions that you have with them. Take risks, be courageous, be sensitive and empathic, and, without being judgmental, let them have space. See the patterns that keep you trapped together in the old ways, and perhaps you will start to talk about them little by little. Maybe your relationships will become more real and, over time, more energetically divine and physically alive.

So let's do one final exploration.

EXPLORATION SESSION

If you are working with a partner, sit across from each other and decide who will be Partner A and who will be Partner B. Then proceed as follows for the first question:

- Partner A asks B the first question.
- Partner B answers, and A says, "Thank you."
- For ten minutes, Partner A continues to ask the question again in a fresh way, as if posing it for the first time, and then thanks B for each answer.
- The roles are now switched: B asks A the first question, again for ten minutes.

For the second question, you will use what we call the looping format:

- A asks B the question and says, "Thank you" after the response.
- B then asks A the question, saying "Thank you" after the response.
- A again asks B, followed by B asking A, and so forth for twenty minutes.

1. Tell me how you experience spirit and world coming together for you.

2. Tell me a way you can more completely express divine eros in your life.

If you are doing this on your own, ask yourself the following questions in contemplation, and take some time to write down your responses.

1. Reflect upon how you experience spirit and world coming together for you.
2. Explore ways you can more completely express divine eros in your life.

Questions and Comments

Student: I found out something in the latest exercise that was totally new when I came from a place of not-knowing. It unfolded itself and it was beautiful. I was surprised about what was coming.

Karen: Not-knowing is one of the ways the mystery expresses itself that lets us have an opening to something that is unknown to come and make itself known. Not-knowing is an important part of the journey because if we are going toward something we know, we are not really open to experiences that we may not know. You can't learn something new if you already think you know it.

Makes you happy, too, doesn't it? Feeling the mystery in the known is being close to the treasure that continues to open to itself. But there is ignorance . . . and there is the not-known.

Hameed: I think it is good to distinguish between the two kinds of not-knowing. The not-knowing of ignorance is when we don't know something because we don't have the information. This is different from the not-knowing that is a state of being, which means that the knowing faculty is at rest. That kind comes about not because we are ignorant but because we trust that we can be in that gap, that stillness. It is not the same as the normal not-knowing, which is, "I don't know; I haven't heard about it." When people here talk about not knowing as an experience, it doesn't mean not-knowing in the sense of not having information.

Student: It's having a deep trust in my inner knowing.

Hameed: Good point; it requires deep trust.

———————

Student: I want to share something from this morning. When I was preparing myself to come here, I was wondering, This blouse or another one . . . pearls on or pearls off . . . *what's the matter?* And when I was walking here, I had all these butterflies in my stomach and I was so nervous. It felt like I was going on a blind date but I had no idea with what or whom. In the meditation, I sat with this incredible nervousness, and then I realized it was a blind date with the unknown and a blind date with myself.

Karen: Did you meet?

Student: I'm still nervous. What I can enjoy already is the quality of open curiosity. And the nervousness is okay.

Karen: Curiosity is very enjoyable. Curiosity is our heart's effect on our mind. Although it is our mind that is interested, it is a heartful interest that is an enjoyment of the process of discovery. We are always in a blind-date situation on our inner journey. We never know how our Beloved is going to be the next minute. The Beloved presents itself in many, many ways. It is always a surprise.

———————

Student: I wish to share in order to understand and to integrate what happened to me, because it feels very overwhelming and important. I couldn't understand the question in this exercise, because it was "How do I express . . ." and I thought it was "How do I experience . . ." I realized that my experience of divine eros has been one of earthly eros, but then suddenly there has been some opening and some beauty and other connections. It felt very much like receiving something from beyond the two of us, but very clearly not something I was expressing. So I struggled with understanding what is "to express."

With help from my partner, we drifted in our looping into a situation where my vision was that I walked close and then surrendered there. It was not me doing and expressing; it felt like it was something that I cannot do but something that happened. After that, a lot of things happened. We stopped asking and we just replied without words to each other. It was so rich and overwhelming. There was first silence, presence, and coming home to the secret garden, really relaxing all my longing, and feeling this is right.

But then came, first in me and then in the woman I was working with, a strong power which was not hard or forceful, not sexual or anything, and then I understood a little bit about the eros part of it. This was a deep experience, but it sort of suggests to me something about the way I can respond now. But I still don't feel that I am expressing anything. It seems like I was there at the edge and something expressed itself, and I'm back to sort of receiving. Do you understand my dilemma?

Karen: You are learning what some kinds of expression can be . . . that something else is expressing itself. It's not the usual you— the expression is part of living. Even in the not-words and not-communication there is an expression. It doesn't mean you have to say it in words. It can be said, but the words don't say it completely. The expression is really the flow through you, in the sense that it is what took over; something was expressing itself through you.

Student: And it didn't feel like I was expressing.

Karen: There was expression, but not you expressing.

Hameed: That is what Karen meant earlier in saying, "We are an organ of expression for reality." In fact, it is always reality expressing itself, but it expresses itself through us, and we think we are expressing ourselves. The expression becomes more profound when we recognize it is not the usual one expressing; something else is expressing itself.

Student: Maybe it will be easier for me to understand now, when I'm back in my life, how to just let myself be expressed.

Karen: Yes, you don't have to try to express yourself. It is a matter of letting that presence inform your expression and form your expression. But in reality, it is not your expression anyway, as you found out.

Hameed: We refer to that function as service. We are of service to the truth. We serve the truth by giving ourselves to the truth to use for its expression. That is how we serve.

Karen: And that is actually another facet of a complete human being. The more complete we are, the more we are in service to our nature. That's an opportunity, and it is also a potential we all have.

Student: I'd like to share how I felt during these days. It's like the most divine feast in my hometown, but not any feast in the regular sense. I felt, right from the beginning, the state in which I was with the issues going on in my life, and how that would combine with divine eros . . . that there was space for everything in that. So I felt like I really could relax because of the structure, or the way it is organized, with your teaching and teachers. All of that together gave this immense freedom and space for me to relax and experience things for myself.

The inner committee I mentioned the other day seemed to have gone on a vacation. But from this morning on, I feel the inner committee is there again, and I feel this trembling for not wanting to leave here. I know it ends, but I don't want to leave it. I feel a sorrow about this field we have and where it is going, even if we say, "Yeah, we take it home with us." But there is such intense energy, and I know that the next time I pass by the road here, it is not the same. It is not the same. Where does it go? This is somehow like an exquisite monastery, but not like a monastery that you would normally think of as a monastery. I'd really like to thank this whole thing.

Karen: Everybody here has contributed to what has happened, and that is the beauty and the value of coming together as a group when we have a like mind, when we love the same thing. That is what nurtures the whole experience and allows it to grow. It is true that as we disperse and go back into our lives, we feel another kind of pull, and that can be frightening; but you do have the ability to stay with and take with you what you've learned.

I felt some sadness this morning about leaving, too. I feel close to all of you. I feel that a very beautiful fountain has been opened up, and that's been a delight. But I also feel that being able to take back what I have learned here and what I have been able to experience with you is very gratifying. And what can arise from the depth of the heart when we feel this way is gratitude. That is something that lives within us—gratitude for the fact that we found another way to know the Beloved.

But the sadness sometimes means that we believe we will leave something here. And it is important to stay with that, because you might feel a loss, and go through it, and do what you can do to be with it . . . and you might find something precious inside of that loss. So, as we leave, we sometimes feel we will lose something or lose what we've gained, but that is another thing that we can look at, use, eat up; it's part of the feast. You have to digest, hang out, let it move through you; part of having a feast is being able to go back in your life and use the nutrients from it.

Hameed: I also want to say that, as Karen pointed out, it is really a collective effort. All of us together open what is called a jump gate. You open a gate in space-time in order to jump into what's beyond it. It is not easy to do this by oneself; it takes a great deal. Here we have been able to open a jump gate to jump beyond our everyday experience to something more profound.

It is true that when you leave here you might wonder, "Where am I going to find a jump gate?" We have been giving you a taste of what happens when a jump gate opens. This is one of the advantages of having a group. It's part of a teaching situation to create a context for that to happen, for that energy to become strong and subtle enough to create the jump gate. As you do the meditation and the inquiry on your own, and perhaps at times with the support of others, in time you may develop your own skill to open a jump gate. It may not be as big as one opened by a whole group, but you will be able to jump beyond time and space by yourself. That is the importance of the practices, and that's why we taught you the belly meditation. We focused on that one because it is something you can continue doing. It is a skill that develops; the more you do it, the better you get at it. It is the same thing with the inquiry—it's a skill you develop.

Student: First I want to express my deep gratefulness for being able to participate in this seminar and for being able to discover divine eros in so many fields that I thought are separated from each other. I feel a big relief and I feel very rich. What I discovered in the last inquiry is that if I experience divine eros and attraction, a pull toward certain things, it is not necessary to have these things, people, or whatever I'm longing for. Actually, sometimes it is enough to enjoy this attraction, this pull, this energy, and doing that creates a lot of space that is starting to be filled. I am really happy and want to thank you both and everybody who is here who contributed to this seminar. It feels like it has a big impact on my life.

Karen: Your life will find out.

Hameed: Eros is smiling.

Karen: Life feels pretty good at the moment.

Student: Yeah, I can feel it smiling . . . it or him! Thank you.

Student: I'd like to tell you about my experience in the last inquiry because it was so surprising. During the looping, my partner was talking about choosing apples and pears. Then it was my turn, and I talked about how it was to give an apple to someone, and the difference when I give a pear to someone. I explained why a pear was more, and then I described the pear. My partner, on her turn, was touched by the way I described the pear, the juiciness and the form. I was describing the juice coming out of it if you just take a little bit of the skin out of it and suck it. The most surprising thing was that I was not aware of the erotic part of it, just the divine part of giving a pear to someone.

As she mentioned that, the juiciness came down from my mouth to my heart, and then the looping went on and I said, "Shall we share the juicy pear?" And so that happened, and then the juiciness went down even more in my body and I really couldn't stop it. It even came out of all my pores, and boy, it was . . .

Karen: Oh, the ecstasy of pears! Fruit will never be the same again.

Student: I'll suck the pear, really?

Karen: May I have a bite? Actually it's a little late to ask . . . it's contagious.

Student: I'm not sure about what I'm going to say. I think it's about the relationship between openness and being closed. I experienced here a lot of difficulty with that, because sometimes I feel a tremendous amount of energy that is stuck in my body. It's like if I'm not open, I feel constant pressure and pain in my body, and for me that's difficult to deal with.

Karen: Do you know what stops it? What makes you not open to let that energy flow? Is it happening right now?

Student: I'm a bit shaky. Maybe fears of disapproval or something. I can't really sense it right now.

Karen: If that were happening to me, I would be interested in finding out what the energy is hitting up against and what is keeping it in place—what the barrier is to letting that come forward. What are you afraid of and what do you think will happen? Or there might be many other things.

Student: There are many things, actually; I am discovering many things.

Hameed: You can start by being open to the stuckness, to the closedness. If you start somewhere else, it will stay closed. You can say, "Okay, I feel closed, I feel stuck—that is how I feel" . . . and you welcome that.

Student: I had one experience here about feeling the emptiness, and somebody asked me, "How do you feel eros?" or something like that. I said, "I don't feel shit" and then I felt it, I entered it right away. It is difficult to deal with pain that is constantly there.

Karen: It sounds like there is not just a stuckness but also a pressure, and you might want to see what that pressure is. When you said "fear of disapproval," I wondered whether you have a lot of internal criticism, if you're judging yourself for it. That is something you need to discover. It sounds as though when you said, "I don't feel shit," you blew that off for a minute. That is one way in which aggression is very important as a creative force in us, for it allows us to create some space and openness where we feel that pressure. The superego, the critic, the committee, or whatever you want to call it, is a pressure of using that force against ourselves and keeping eros repressed.

Student: I sometimes felt it during the course, like when I feel it's like a lie and then . . . Aaarggh! [*student makes a loud sound*]. . . then it feels better right away.

Karen: How about now?

Student: Yeah, when I do that, it feels already a bit better. I feel a bit away, not here in a way.

Karen: You go away, kind of?

Student: I feel a bit high, not really on the ground.

Karen: What happens if you put the microphone down and go "Aaarggh!" and feel your belly? Stay with your belly while you're doing it.

Student: I did it yesterday already.

Karen: Did it work?

Hameed: I'd like to hear it.

Student: Without the microphone . . . Aaarggh!

Hameed: We are a very accepting committee.

Student: It's okay . . . it's enough now.

Karen: What are you feeling now?

Student: I'm glad. I was so nervous to do this; my heart was beating, jumping out of me. But it feels actually very good to look at everybody.

Karen: What are you feeling in your body?

Student: I feel that my tension is here. [*pointing to head*]

Karen: What's happening down here? [*pointing to belly and legs*]

Student: My legs are shaking a bit less right now. I find it difficult to feel them.

Karen: How about in your heart?

Student: I laugh a lot, but that feeling of heart laughter . . . it has been a while since I really felt it. And during one session with somebody, I really felt it, and today also for a short moment. Now I don't really feel a strong sensation there.

Karen: After you allowed yourself to make that sound, you looked fuller. You looked like a lioness.

Student: It's so funny. Yesterday I was going back home after I growled, and I was thinking, ". . . like an animal." I was on the train, and I opened my eyes and there was a huge billboard with a lion looking at me. And this morning, when I looked at myself on the train, I saw an animal, completely wild.

Karen: Thank you. Our wildness combined with our angelic nature makes us become a wild angel, where the wildness of the animal is not simply about the satisfaction of desires. It is the wild energy of the body and the delightful and heavenly, all as one unified energy in service of the truth.

Student: I'd like to share something that I'm excited about. It's invoked by something you said in the talk about how life is everywhere showing itself in all the experiences that are here. I feel very excited how I can feel that life is coming to me and showing itself in many forms and in what I do 99 percent of the time. I usually don't want to be in those forms; I say, "No, no, no, not that!" and I want to be elsewhere. I realize I don't have to do anything because it's coming all the time and I just have to listen and let it come to me. Yeah!

Karen: How do you feel?

Student: I feel very shaky.

Karen: Ecstasy always makes us tremble. You look happy.

Student: Yeah . . . Yeah . . . Gosh.

Hameed: "Yeah" sounds good.

Student: There is something about it that I would like to say. My experience of life energy is that when it is moving through me, the shakiness happens. I feel it as if it is invading me, and my reaction to it is that I'm getting penetrated. It's something outside of me that gets into my body and bodily sensations; and even allowing and listening, just listening, it's . . . let me say . . . it can feel like having sex.

Karen: Yeah.

Student: Being with that, I'm very excited to go into my life and see what's there, especially in my own experiences of anger, fear, crying, and tenseness and all the things that I don't want to allow. My gosh, what's it going to bring? What is there?

Karen: More of that!

Hameed: Sounds good. As you see, it can bring up many things in our unconscious—fears and excitement alike.

Student: What a rush.

Hameed: You will have an erotic adventure with life. You don't know what's going to happen with an adventure. That's what's exciting about it.

Karen: That's the thrill.

Student: It's so amazing that I don't have to do anything . . . it's coming all the time.

Karen: That's the truth, isn't it? If we try to make something like that happen, it doesn't. You have to let it happen. We learn to be open to it. We come to understand what is in the way, and then it is a natural occurrence.

Student: And even not wanting to let it happen is okay . . . and that's there too. Good.

Student: This morning I was waking up and my wife started to caress me, and then later on, tears came out of me and I got in touch with this child longing for his mother. I saw it has so much power, but this power has been turned against the whole world. I couldn't stop my crying. For years, I was looking for this point where something real could happen with the child. I'm pretty much thankful to feel the power and turn it somewhere else instead of all the hate I have toward people and toward myself. This is the state I am in now. Yes, and thank you for helping me come to this point. It is not easy for me to be in groups like this and to share it with you. Thank you.

Hameed: I'm glad you shared it with us; I appreciate your sharing with us something significant even though it is difficult to share. Many people experience their inner child coming up, the child that has been limited and constricted and scared . . . or whatever way we have held on to the child. The child needs to come up so that it will be touched by the real energy that can transform it and make it become more part of us, part of what we are, what we experience of ourselves.

Karen: Much of what keeps us from being able to go to a new level of maturity is this part of us that we feel as a child. This part of us holds many of the painful experiences and difficulties we have had, but also things that we hold precious. Some aspects of our essence are held captive in the form of a child in our psyche. We often feel that letting go of that innocent, childlike part means that we will lose our heart qualities, but as we understand and embrace that little one, our loving acceptance melts the child's boundaries, and those qualities become part of who we are. Our heart becomes free and mature. It doesn't have to remain in the image of that little child. Our childhood was often the last time we felt in touch with that kind of presence.

This seminar most likely brought up various kinds of things from our history—and the child of our history in particular—because often that's what we are identified with emotionally. So it seems like you are in the process of seeing that little boy and embracing him. That is important for all of us, actually.

Hameed: I have an idea. I was feeling gratitude—feeling grateful for being with you here and for everybody sharing and receiving the sharing. I think many people here are feeling gratitude for the situation or the opportunity, and I want us all to express our gratitude together in an ending ceremony.

It has been wonderful being with all of you, being with the situation here and being in a beautiful city, and in good weather, too. It is good to hear the different things that are happening, to see you all dealing with the challenges and being able to jump to the next place in your unfolding. As I said before, this seminar has been created and supported by many people, not only by Karen and me. Karen and I are the ones who are presenting the teaching, but we have our organizers and our teachers who have been available and supporting each meeting before and afterward; the sound crew, the people who carry the mikes . . . it's the whole situation really. And most important is our true nature, the source of all we are grateful for.

So I would like us to end by expressing our gratitude in an OM salutation, giving our gratitude to our true nature and to everybody who made this possible, including all of you. And after that, we want to respect that gratitude and feel it as we walk out in silence, leaving the space with gratitude and peace in it.

About the Diamond Approach

The Diamond Approach is taught by Ridhwan teachers, ordained by the Ridhwan Foundation to be its ministers. They are trained by the Ridhwan Foundation, through an extensive seven-year program, which is in addition to their work and participation as students of the Diamond Approach. The ordination process ensures that each person has a good working understanding of the Diamond Approach and a sufficient capacity to teach it before being ordained and authorized to be a Ridhwan teacher.

The Diamond Approach described in this book is taught in group and private settings in the United States, Canada, Europe, Australia, and New Zealand by Ridhwan teachers. For information about the various contexts for pursuing this work, we invite you to visit www.ridhwan.org.

If you would like to explore starting a group in your area, taught by ordained Ridhwan teachers, write:

Ridhwan
P.O. Box 2747
Berkeley, CA 94702-0747

For more information on the books of A. H. Almaas, go to www.ahalmaas.com.

DIAMOND APPROACH and RIDHWAN are trademarks or registered trademarks of the Ridhwan Foundation.

Index

Abbott, Edwin, 110
aloneness, 66–67
Amsterdam, the scintillating journey
  in, 6–8
Amsterdam seminar, 3–4
angel and animal, uniting, 147, 182–83,
  193–94, 212, 222
anger, 20–21
animal and angel, uniting. *See* angel
  and animal, uniting
attachment, 8, 15, 54, 55, 75, 90, 177, 183
attraction. *See under* love
attunement, 119–20, 125, 136–37, 146

being present. *See* presence
belly center
  awakening of, 202–3
  awareness of, 12, 160
  developing, 50
  eros and, 10, 140
  life force and, 10
  meditations on, 10, 11
  overview, 10, 160, 208
  See also spiritual centers
Beloved, 80–82, 108, 143, 211, 212, 215, 218
  continual discovery of new things
    about one's, 148
  desire and erotic love for inner, 3, 55,
    162, 203–4

intimacy with, 133, 135
intimate friendship as reflecting the
  true, 3
loving desire toward our essential
  nature as the, 91
music as window to inner, 199
seeing the world as the face of our
  inner, 210
union with, 5, 91, 165, 170, 192, 204 (*see*
  also union)
See also love: falling in; source
Big Bang, 59
body, 154–55
  and the divine, 154–55
body centers. *See* spiritual centers
boundaries, 25, 45
  creating, 44, 45
  fear of letting go of, 66, 67
  feeling like there are no, 153–54
  love melting, 49, 165, 204, 224
  nature of, 45, 153
  See also union; unity
brains. *See* spiritual centers

chakras. *See* spiritual centers
chanting, 51, 135, 181–82
childbirth, 161, 162
Christian mystical writings, erotic
  language in, 150

committee, inner. *See* superego
consciousness
  divine eros and, 13
  waves in the ocean of, 109–11
control, losing, 146. *See also* surrender
courage, 65
critic, inner. *See* superego
Cupid, 25
Cupid's arrow, 25, 27
curiosity, 215. *See also* mystery: love of

death and dying, 127–28, 161
dependency, 89
desire, 25
  embracing and experiencing, 25 (*see
    also* emotions: suppressing vs.
    being with)
  embracing the experience of vs. the
    object of one's, 82
  energy of, 76, 79, 82, 85–91, 203–4 (*see
    also* energy, pure)
  as the expression of the true energy
    of Being, 83
  and feeling alive, 79
  feeling of pure, 80
  feelings about, 73–74
  freedom from, 25
  freeing desire from the past, 73–77
  vs. grasping, 90 (*see also* neediness)
  lack and, 75–78, 81, 86, 88 (*see also*
    emptiness)
  nature of, 74–75, 78–83, 86
  from soul vs. egoistic sources, 88 (*see
    also* ego desire/egoistic desire)
  spirituality and, 16
  See also *specific topics*
dialectic inquiry, 105, 124–25, 130–32, 136,
    172, 212
  defined, 105
  erotic dimension, 141, 151
  nature of, 125
Diamond Approach, 6, 140, 227
  actualization and realization, 96
  body centers and, 10

eros and sexuality in, 140
goal/purpose, 2–3, 12–13
inquiry in, 19, 52
inquiry into ordinary experience,
    52, 66
meditation practices in, 9, 52
overview, 6, 140
spirituality in, 2–3, 9, 12, 59
Diamond Approach teachers, 47
distance, 57–58, 186–87. *See also* time and
    space
divine
  and the body, 154–55
  illuminating the, 12–15
  and the instinctual, 147
  meanings and connotations of, 14–15,
    18, 23
divine eros, 145–49, 162
  definition and meaning of, 13, 60, 155
  energy of, 171
  experiences of, 155
  finding new ways to open up the
    field to, 151–52
  paradox of, 15–17
  See also *eros; specific topics*
dualism, 91
duality, 62–65. *See also* loving, division
    and polarity in; one; reality: one;
    spirit: world and; unity

ego, 1–2, 72, 75–77. *See also* "I"
ego desire/egoistic desire, 74–77, 88, 89
egolessness, 14, 15, 64. *See also* "I,"
    disappearance of the
emotions
  suppressing vs. being with, 7, 20, 75,
    84, 85, 88–89, 206
  understanding, 20–21
  See also *heart*
empathy for the other, 118–20, 125,
    136–39, 184
emptiness, 59, 68, 77, 78, 207
  exploring deficient, 77–82
  See also *stillness*

energy, pure, 7, 76, 79, 84, 165, 211–12
eros, 7
    awakening, 143–46
    desire and, 74
    distortion of, 183–85
    and the divine, 7, 14, 23–24, 147 (*see also*
        divine eros)
    finding new ways to express, 151–52
    is always pure and divine, 7
    many faces of, 140–43
    meanings, 24, 60
    mission, 61
    sex and, 140–41, 149–51
    spirit and, 2, 32
Eros (God), 53, 61
erotic, 23–24
    exploring what limits your
        experience of the, 151
    meanings, 149–50
erotic love, 74, 149, 152. *See also* loving,
    division and polarity in
eternity, one in, 17–18
Exploration Sessions, 22–23, 42–43,
    62–63, 85–86, 102–5, 123–26, 151–52, 172,
    194–95, 213–14
expression, 96, 186–87, 214–16
    of eros, 140–42, 173
    of one consciousness appearing as
        many, 166
    of our spiritual nature, 136
    See also spiritual centers

fear, 63, 155
    of letting go of boundaries, 66, 67
    of unity, 184–86
feedback loops, 121, 137–40, 150
    defined, 121, 138
    See also looping
feelings. *See* desire; emotions
Flatland (Abbott), 110
fountain of love/bliss, 27, 28, 165, 218
freedom, 1, 8, 34–36, 40–42, 54, 56, 96, 210
    from charge to, 205–7
    expression and, 96 (*see also* expression)

love of, 34, 35
    sexuality and, 148
    spiritual, 34, 36, 39, 43–44, 47–48, 56
    true inner, 96
    wisdom and, 211
    See also under desire; friendship
friendship, 103, 126–30, 137
    creating a birth canal through, 162
    desire for union in, 186
    eroticism in, 125–26, 130, 141, 148–51, 162
    and mutuality in the relational field,
        121–23
    openness and freedom in, 126, 148–49
    types of, 186–87
    See also loves of the heart

Gestalt therapy, 80–81
giving, 24
God, 14, 41, 55, 59, 101
    desire for intimacy and unity with,
        92, 170, 190, 195
    love and, 54, 154, 190, 198
    meanings of, 14
    sensual experience with, 150
    spiritual centers and, 208
    union with, 5
    See also Eros
grounding center, 10. *See also* belly
    center
Gurdjieff, George Ivanovich, 208

hara, 10. *See also* belly center
head center, 10, 152, 159–60, 208. *See also*
    spiritual centers
heart, 40
    two loves of the, 32–38
    See also emotions; love; loving
heart center, 10, 156, 160, 208. *See also*
    spiritual centers
hormones, 163–64
HU (mantra), 51, 135, 181
human being, becoming a complete, 117
human nature, 18, 34, 155. *See also* true
    nature

"I," disappearance of the, 59, 70. *See also*
   egolessness
Ibn 'Arabi, 150
inquiry
   defined, 19
   into ordinary experience, 52, 66
   the practice of, 19–22
instinct and the divine, 147, 182–83,
   193–94. *See also* animal and angel
intimacy, 63, 132–33, 135, 142, 189
   desire for, 141–42 (*see also under* God)
invisible world, finding the, 52

judgment, 80, 84, 177. *See also* superego

Kath meditation, 10–12, 135, 160, 176
   OM salutation and, 31, 159
knowledge. *See* mystery; not-knowing
kundalini, 178

lack and desire, 75–78, 81, 86, 88. *See also*
   emptiness
life, love of, 34
Living Being
   awakening to, 208
   expression and celebration of, 81, 211
looping, 140, 143, 150, 216, 219–20
   defined, 121
   between heart and mind, 205
   See also feedback loops
looping format, 213
love, 80–81, 154, 193
   the attraction called, 188–89
   dimensions of, 72
   falling in, 26–27, 37, 49, 75, 76, 165, 171,
      188, 192–93, 203, 204 (*see also* Beloved;
      union)
   God and, 54, 154, 190, 198
   nature of, 36–38, 45–46, 48–49, 60
   opens the door to reality and our
      deeper nature, 7
   passionate desire and, 16–18, 22–27, 53,
      74, 87, 141, 151–52
   the presence of, 38–42

See also heart; selfless love
loves of the heart, two, 32–38
loving, division and polarity in, 53–56,
   151–52, 156

magnetism, 189–91
material world. *See* loving; spirit:
   world and
meditation experience with one's true
   nature, 150–51
meditation(s), 201
   on belly center, 10, 11
   in Diamond Approach, 9, 52
   See also Kath meditation; music
      meditations; practice
mind and heart
   the dance of, 5–6
   love affair between, 6–7
miracles and reality, 112–13
music meditations, 49–50, 91–92, 132–33,
   156–57, 160, 199
mystery, 56, 189, 197, 214
   love of, 33–34, 170 (*see also* curiosity)
   of unity, 188–89, 192, 194

neediness, 73, 76, 81, 84, 89, 90
nonattachment, 8. *See also* attachment
not-knowing, 214–15. *See also* mystery
now, feeling the presence of, 39. *See also*
   presence

OM salutation, 31, 159, 160, 225
one
   in eternity, 17–18
   See also reality: one; unity
One
   integrating it all into, 209–13
   two as, 185–87
open-hearted field, 160–63
openness
   in relationships, 78, 97, 99–102, 118,
      126–27, 130, 132, 137–39, 144, 145, 148–49,
      162, 212
   selfless love and, 78
orgasm, 143, 156–57

pain, 93–94, 98–99, 106, 183, 195–96
empathizing with another's, 118
of humanity, 195
love and, 191
physical, 47
See also suffering
passion, 24
path (Zen), 52
pelvic center, 152, 156. *See also* spiritual centers
personal contact, discovering, 99–102
physical world. *See* spirit: world and practice
importance of continued, 202–5
See also meditation practices
presence, 9–10, 20, 39
cannot be contained, 40
of love, 38–42
primordial existence, 17, 18
procreation
drive for, 163–65
See also childbirth
puberty, 163

Quasar Seminars, 2–4
culture and nature working together, 4–5
the dance of mind and heart, 5–6

real relationship
definition and nature of, 114–15, 136–37
opening up the, 113–18
reality
living in, 61–63
making love with, 150–51
one, 56–64
realization, 117
relating, the challenge of, 94–97
relational field, 114–17, 119–20, 125–26, 139, 212
mutuality in the, 120–23
nature of, 113, 121
See also open-hearted field
relational sensitivity, 136–37

relationship(s)
developing, 135–40
difficulties in erotic, 145
divine and sexual dimensions of erotic, 142
openness in, 78, 97, 99–102, 118, 126–27, 130, 132, 137–39, 144, 145, 148–49, 162, 212
spiritual nature of, 97–99
See also friendship; real relationship; *specific topics*
religion, 41–42, 150
Rode Hoed, 4
Rumi, 150

self, 79. *See also* "I"
self-centeredness, 14–16, 79, 142–43
self-esteem/self-worth, 48–49
selfless love, 22, 48, 98
desire and, 16–18, 22, 23, 25, 26, 53, 61
divine eros and, 15, 18, 141
and the erotic, 141–43, 145
magnetic love and, 191
openness and, 78
selflessness, 15, 79, 147
desire and, 25, 61, 142, 143, 145
sensitivity, 136–37
separateness, dissolution of, 186. *See also* boundaries; union; unity
service, 217
"sexual," 150
sexual encounters, 146–50, 162, 189
one-night stands, 146
with vs. without true love, 142–43
See also orgasm
sexual energy, 162–64
as the drive that opens us, 163–65
See also *specific topics*
sexuality, sacred, 155. *See also* divine eros; eros: spirit and
sexy angel, 194, 212, 222. *See also* angel
Song of Songs, 150
source, 82
exploding into the, 82–85
space and time, 33–34, 148

beyond, 186–87, 197–98, 218–19
  See also distance
spirit, 58, 98, 148
  eros and, 2, 32 (*see also* eros)
  as impersonal, 98
  world and, 42, 46, 53–63, 69, 108, 148 (*see
    also* loving, division and polarity in)
spiritual centers (body centers), 6, 7, 10,
    152, 159–60, 207–9
spiritual experiences, 58–59. See also
  specific topics
spiritual life, 61–62. See also *specific topics*
spirituality, nature of, 16, 45
stillness, 67–70, 192, 207, 214. *See also*
  emptiness
suffering, 46, 47
  allowing oneself to experience, 94
  causes of, 46, 55, 93–95
  desire, attachment, and, 90 (*see also*
    attachment)
  desire for relief from, 54, 191–92
  ego existence and, 1
  spirituality and, 45, 46
  See also pain
Sufi poetry, 150
superego, 41, 62–64, 80, 221. *See also*
  judgment
surrender, 146, 173

t'an tien, 10. *See also* belly center
tantra, 6
  defined, 6
tantric relationships, 212
tantric way, 7, 206
Taylor, Jill Bolte, 69–70
time and space, 33–34, 148
  beyond, 186–87, 197–98, 218–19
  See also distance
true nature, 60, 96, 164
  communion with our, 207
  discovery of and awakening to our, 108

ego keeps us disconnected from
    our, 77
  experiencing the lack of connection
    to our, 78
  gratitude for our, 225
  individual consciousness and, 190
  melting into our, 173–74
  nature of, 17, 58, 78, 192
  qualities of our, 96, 98, 146
  relationships and, 77, 98, 101–2, 107, 139,
    165, 190, 192
  spirit/spiritual nature as, 15, 58, 185
  two sides of our, 78
  union with our, 165
  unity of our, 181
  See also human nature

unification, celebration of, 155
unified field theory, 193
union
  desire for, 165–68, 170–71 (*see also*
    Beloved: union with)
  divine, 168–70
  See also boundaries; one; One
unity, 181, 185
  fear of, 184–86
  and the passion to reunite, 170–71
  the pull of divine, 189–91
  the truth of, 191–95
  See also Beloved: union with;
    boundaries; one; One

van Eyck, P. N., 197
vulnerability, 174
  defined, 101
  in relationships, 101, 105, 139, 145, 167,
    182, 190

wormholes, 148

Zen, 52, 66